1950s

Ten Years of Popular Hits Arranged for **EASY PIANO**

Arranged by Dan Coates

DECADE by DECADE

Contents

ARRIVEDERCI ROMA

The famous American tenor and Hollywood movie star, Mario Lanza, sang "Arrivederci Roma" in the 1958 film *Seven Hills of Rome*. The young street dweller who appears in the scene was hand-picked by Lanza while filming in Rome. The song's English lyrics were penned by Carl Sigman, the American lyricist and songwriter who is noted for his collaborations with Johnny Mercer, Duke Ellington, and Glenn Miller.

Italian Words by Pietro Garinei and Sandro Giovannini
English Words by Carl Sigman

Music by Renato Rascel
Arranged by Dan Coates

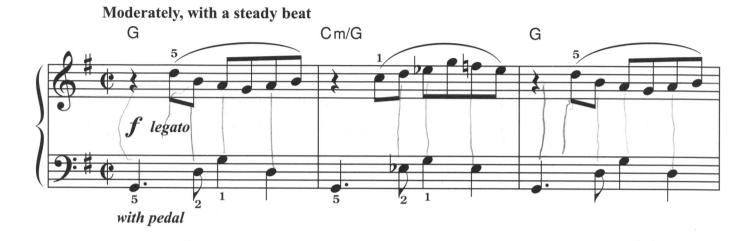

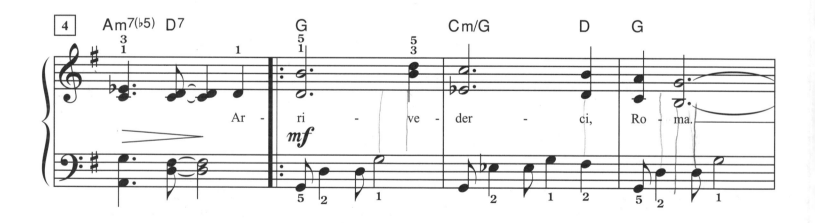

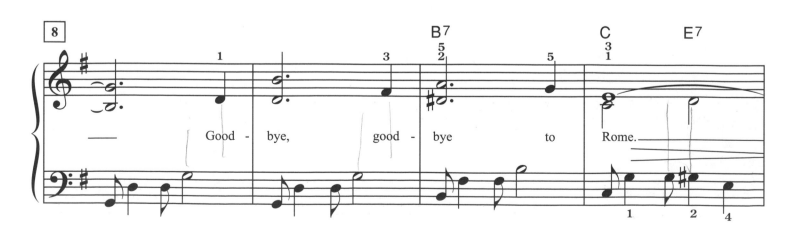

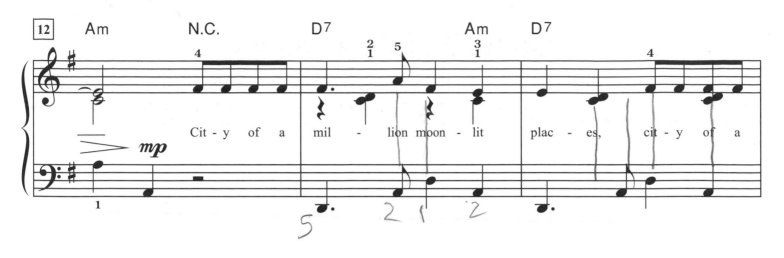

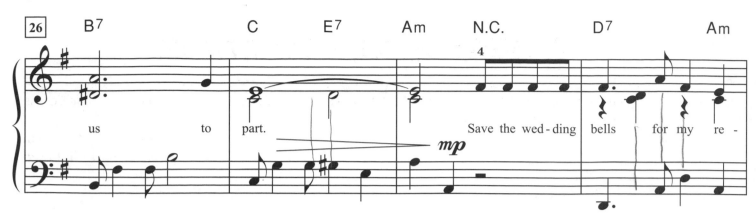

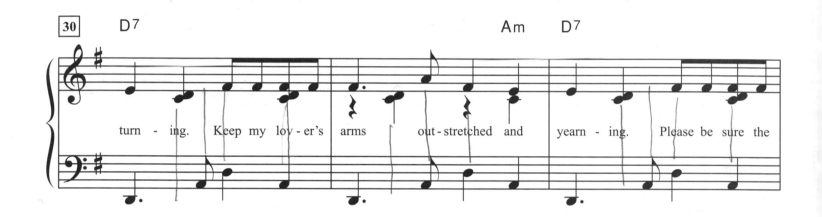

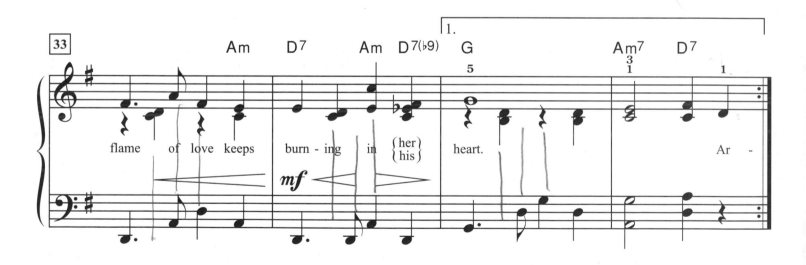

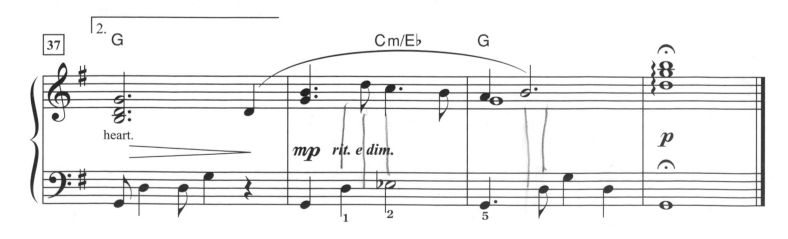

THE BEST IS YET TO COME

"The Best Is Yet to Come" has been recorded by many artists including Tony Bennett, Peggy Lee, Sarah Vaughan, Ella Fitzgerald, Michael Bublé and more. However, it is most often associated with Frank Sinatra. In fact, the words "The Best Is Yet to Come" are imprinted on Sinatra's tombstone.

Music by Cy Coleman
Lyric by Carolyn Leigh
Arranged by Dan Coates

The best is yet to come — and, babe, won't it be fine,

you think you've seen the sun — but you ain't seen it shine.

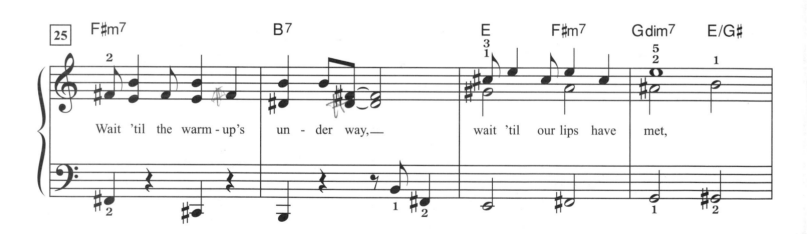

Wait 'til the warm-up's un - der way, — wait 'til our lips have met,

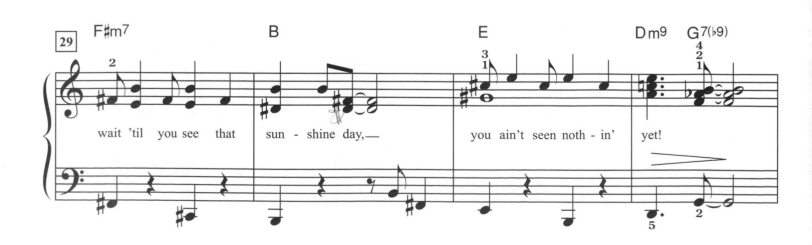

wait 'til you see that sun - shine day, — you ain't seen noth - in' yet!

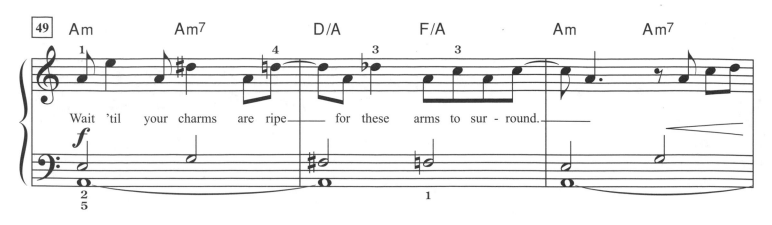

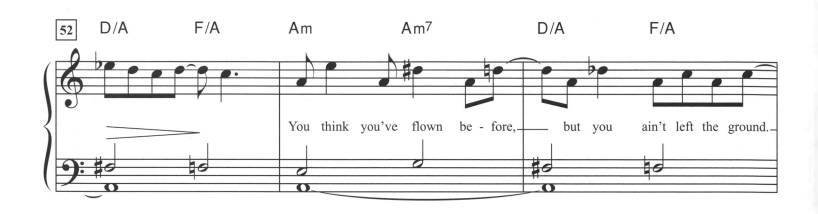

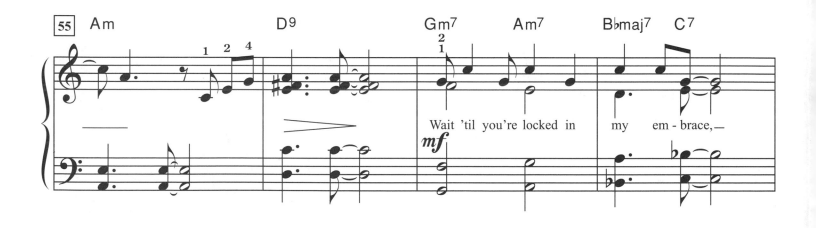

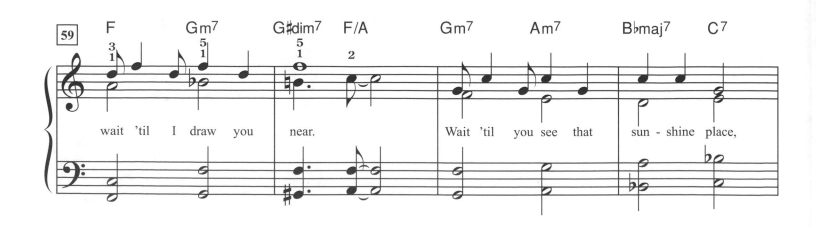

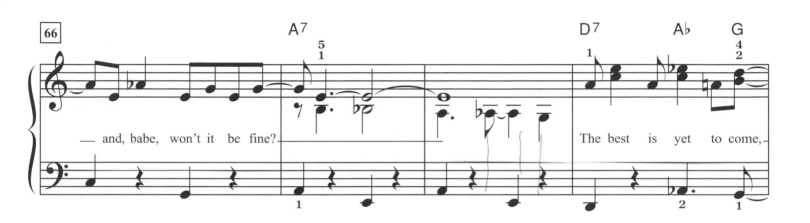

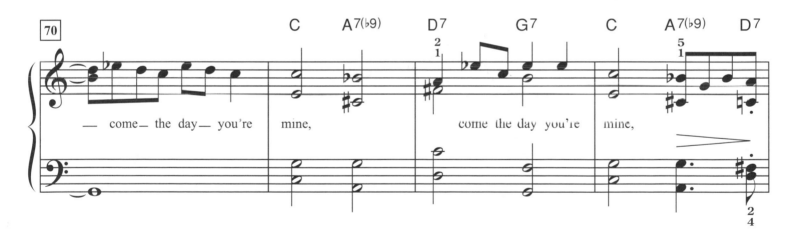

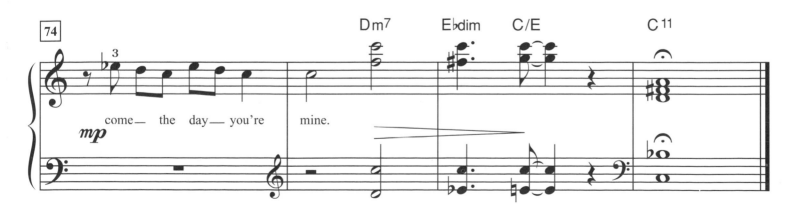

BLUEBERRY HILL

While the sheet music was first published in 1940 and the first recording was released in 1941, "Blueberry Hill" became an international hit when Fats Domino recorded it in 1956. In the popular 1970s sitcom *Happy Days*, which took place in the 1950s, lead character Richie Cunningham (Ron Howard) would often sing the first line of the song when he saw a pretty girl.

Words and Music by
Al Lewis, Vincent Rose and Larry Stock
Arranged by Dan Coates

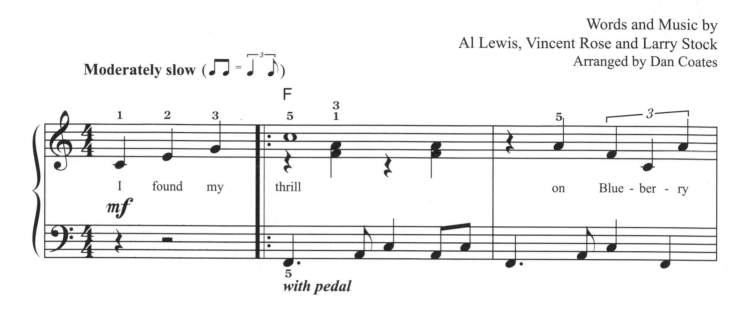

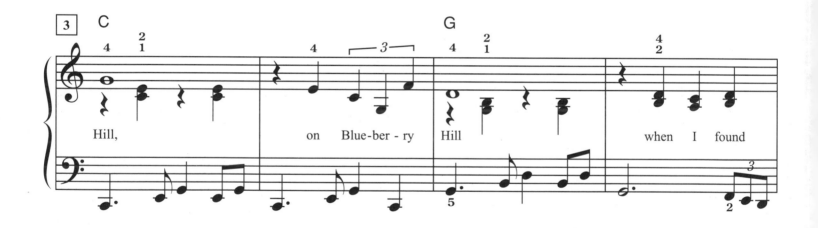

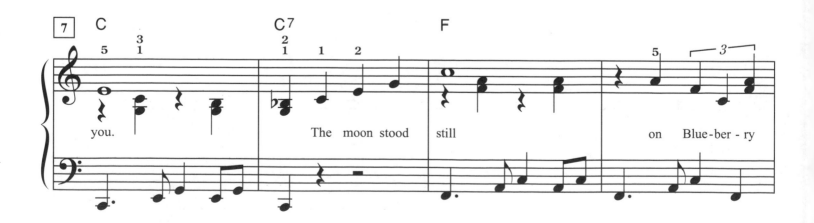

be. Though we're a - part, you're part of me

still for you were my thrill

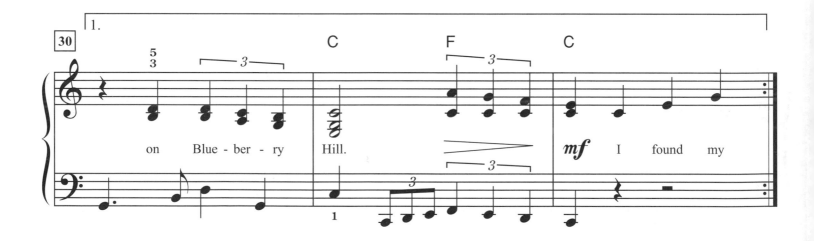

on Blue - ber - ry Hill. *mf* I found my

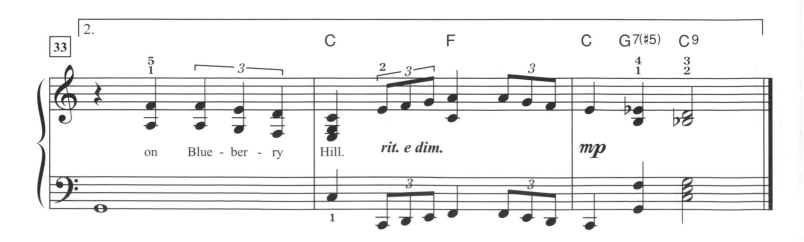

on Blue - ber - ry Hill. *rit. e dim.* *mp*

CARA MIA

1/28/10

The Italian phrase "Cara Mia" means "My Beloved." First published in 1954, "Cara Mia" enjoyed many years on the pop charts starting with a recording by United Kingdom singer David Whitfield, all the way through the 1965 version by Jay and the Americans. Jay and the Americans are best known for their hits "This Magic Moment" and "Come a Little Bit Closer."

Original Words and Music by Tulio Trapani and Lee Lange
Italian lyrics by Gagis
Arranged by Dan Coates

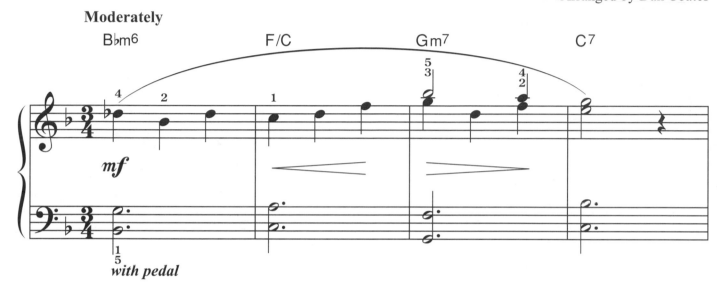

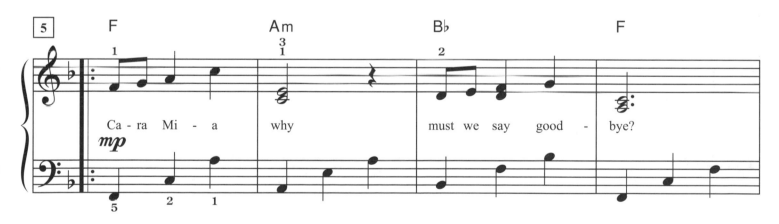

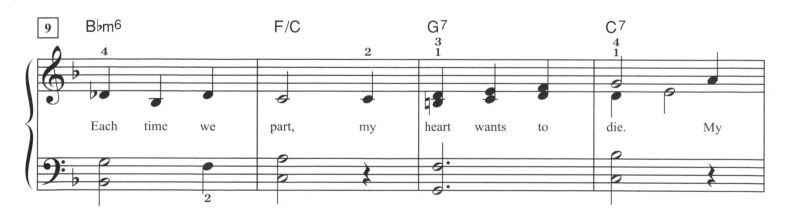

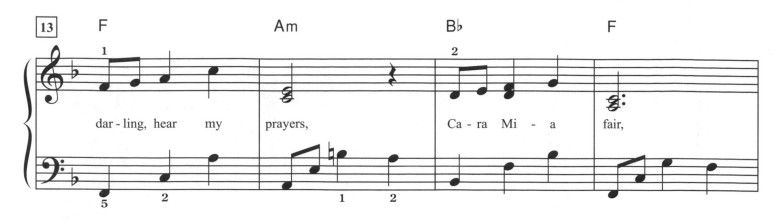

dar - ling, hear my prayers, Ca - ra Mi - a fair,

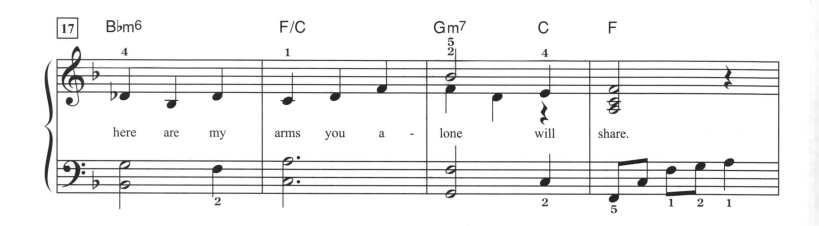

here are my arms you a - lone will share.

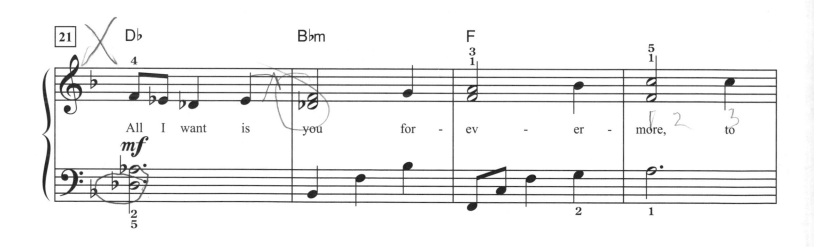

All I want is you for - ev - er - more, to

have, to hold, to love, a - dore.

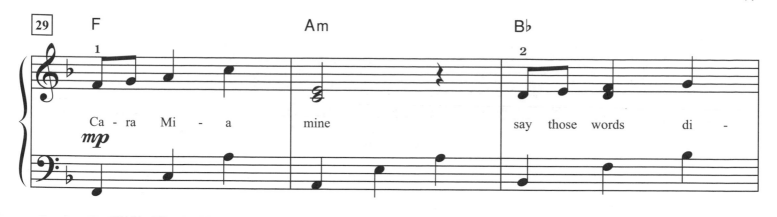

Ca - ra Mi - a mine   say those words di -

vine,   I'll   be   your   love   till   the

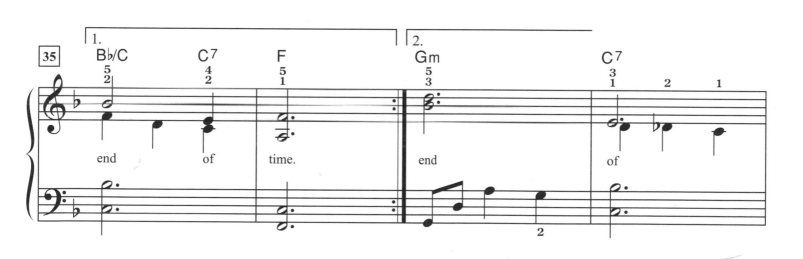

end   of   time.   end   of

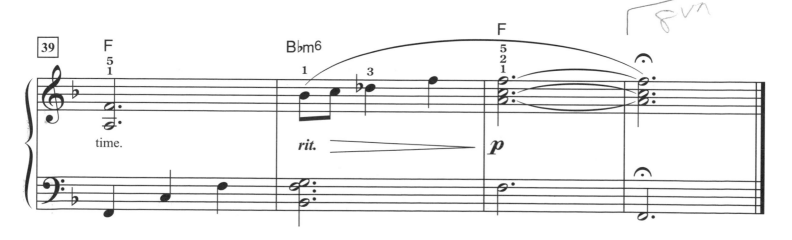

time.   rit. ————————— p

CATCH A FALLING STAR

"Catch a Falling Star" was recorded by the famous crooner, Perry Como. Originally born Pierino Ronald Como, he went on to become one of the most successful performers and recording artists of all time. In fact, it is said that Como had such significant record sales, he told his record company to stop trying to keep track of his sales figures. At the height of his fame, he produced a weekly variety show which set the precedent for future shows in that genre.

Words and Music by Paul Vance and Lee Pockriss
Arranged by Dan Coates

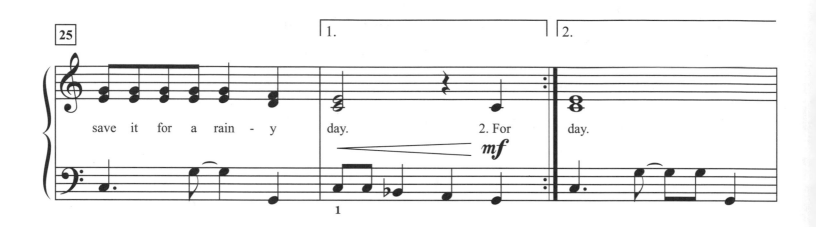

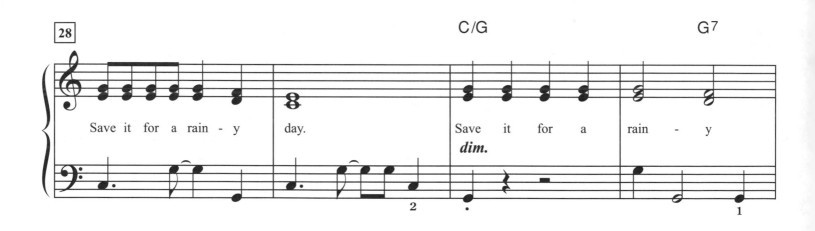

A CERTAIN SMILE

A young and still relatively unknown Johnny Mathis sang "A Certain Smile" in the 1958 movie of the same name. In the movie, he played the role of a nightclub singer. While the movie was not a huge hit, Mathis and his "velvet voice" went on to become one of the biggest recording artists from the 1950s through the 1980s.

By Sammy Fain and Paul Francis Webster
Arranged by Dan Coates

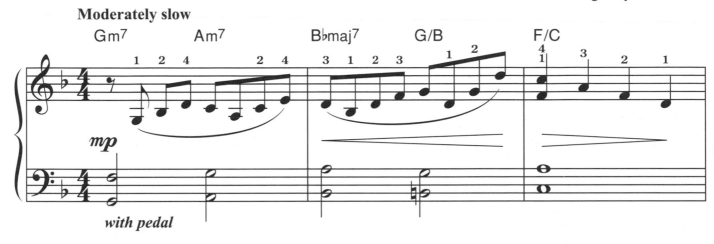

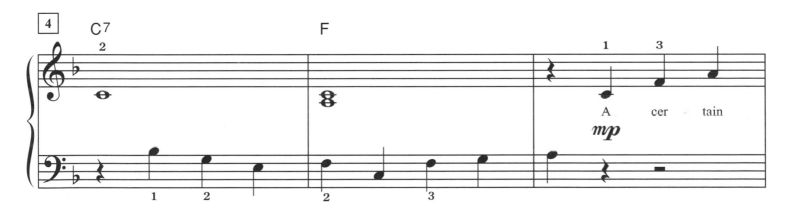

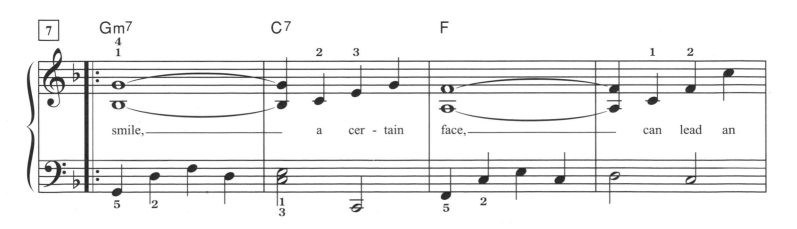

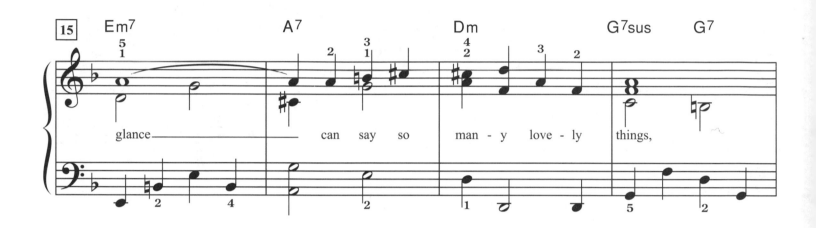

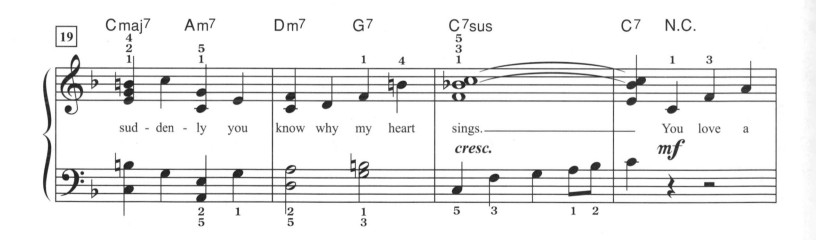

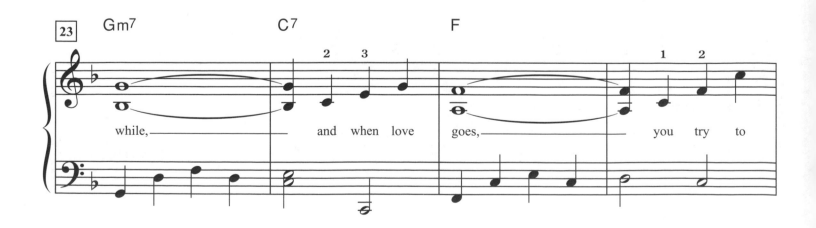

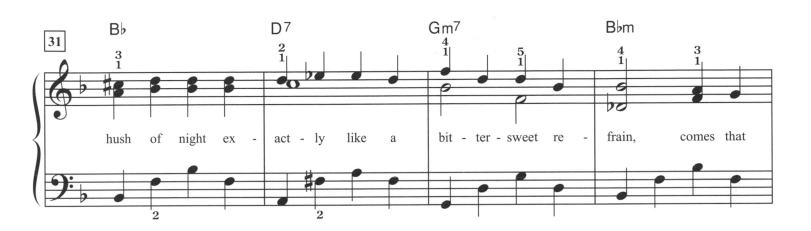

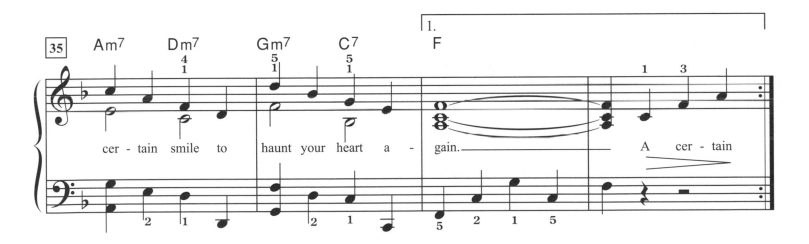

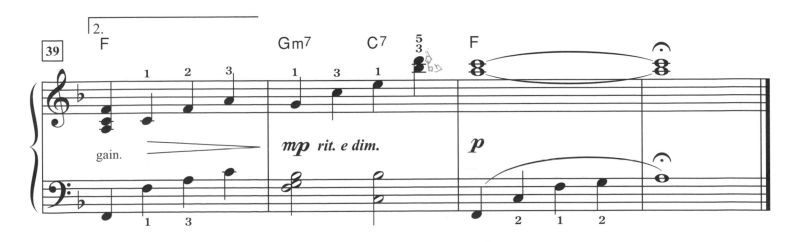

EARTH ANGEL
(WILL YOU BE MINE)

"Earth Angel (Will You Be Mine)" was originally released by The Penguins as the B-side to "Hey Señorita." It quickly gained more popularity than its A-side pairing, and reached #1 on the Billboard charts in 1955. While "Earth Angel" is on Rolling Stone Magazine's list of the 500 Greatest Songs of All Time, it proved to be the only major hit from The Penguins. Because of its popularity, it has been featured in many movies, television shows, and Broadway musicals.

Words and Music by Jesse Belvin
Arranged by Dan Coates

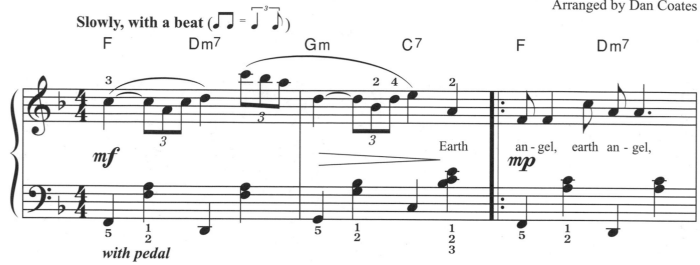

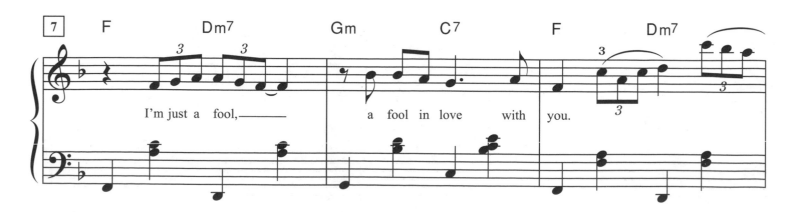

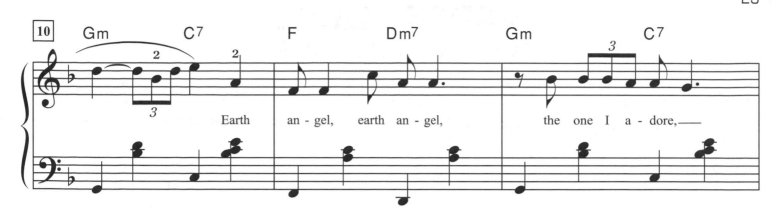

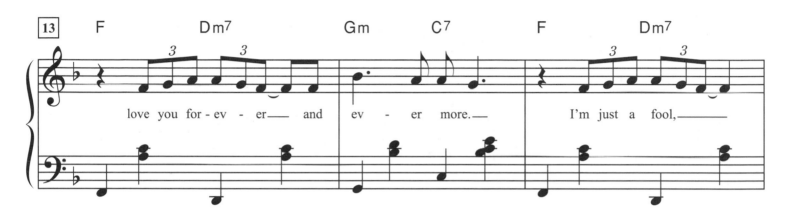

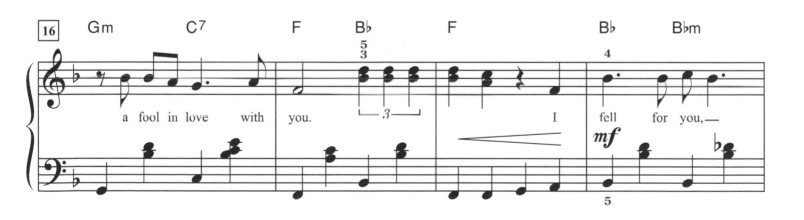

that some-day— I'll be the vi-sion of your— hap-pi- ness. Earth

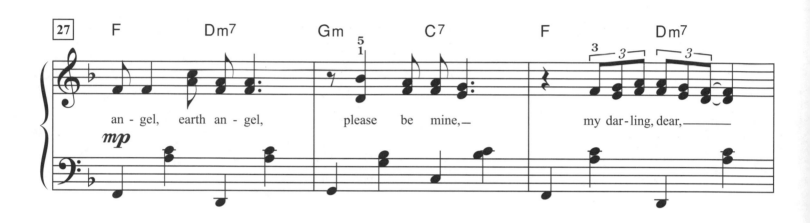

an - gel, earth an - gel, please be mine,— my dar-ling, dear,———

mp

love you— all the time.— I'm just a fool,——— a fool in love with

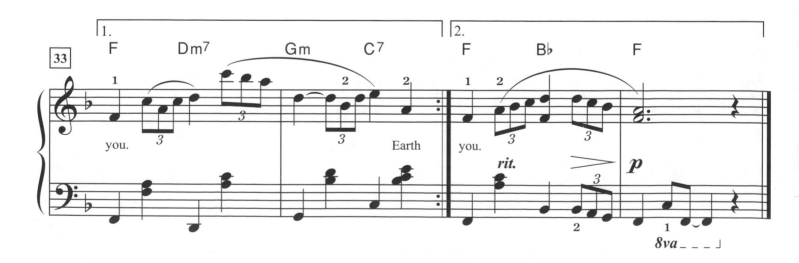

you. Earth you.

rit. *p*

8va

FLY ME TO THE MOON

"Fly Me to the Moon" was written in 1954 and debuted in cabaret shows by singer Felicia Sanders. The song was originally titled "In Other Words," and only later was changed to "Fly Me to The Moon." While Frank Sinatra's 1964 recording is considered by many to be the "classic" version, many singers have put their spin on it, including: Tony Bennett, Paul Anka, Nat King Cole, Perry Como, Bobby Darin, Doris Day, Ella Fitzgerald, Judy Garland, Diana Krall, Wes Montgomery, Sarah Vaughn, Tom Jones, Nancy Wilson, Dinah Washington, Oscar Peterson, Michael Bolton, and many others.

Words and Music by Bart Howard
Arranged by Dan Coates

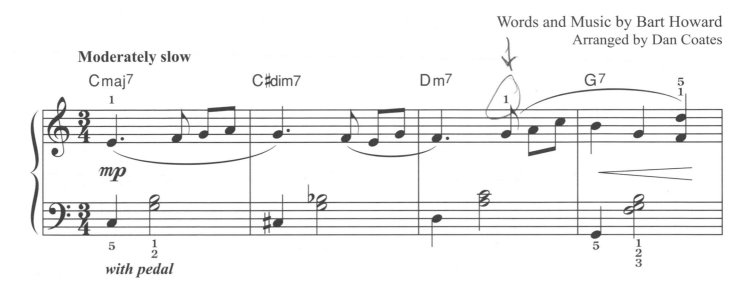

Fly me to the moon, and let me play a-mong the stars.

Let me see what spring is like on Ju - pi - ter and Mars. In

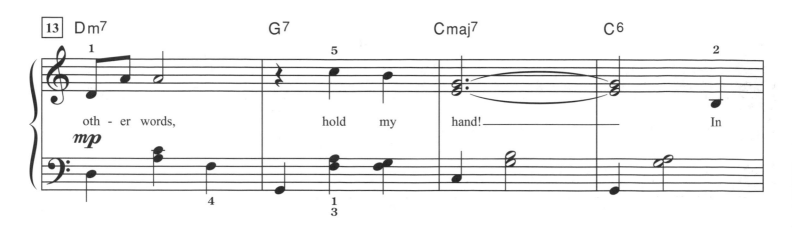

oth - er words,   hold my hand!   In

mp

oth - er words,   dar - ling, kiss me!

Fill   my heart with song   and let me sing   for - ev - er more;

mf

you   are all I long   for, all I wor - ship and a - dore.   In

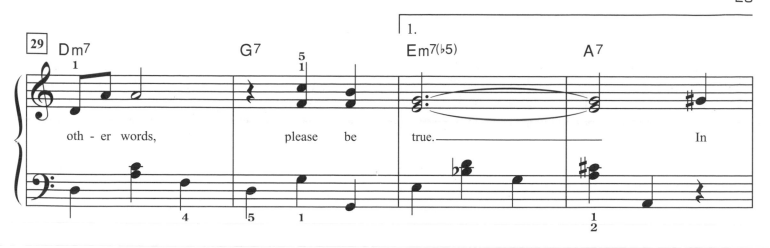

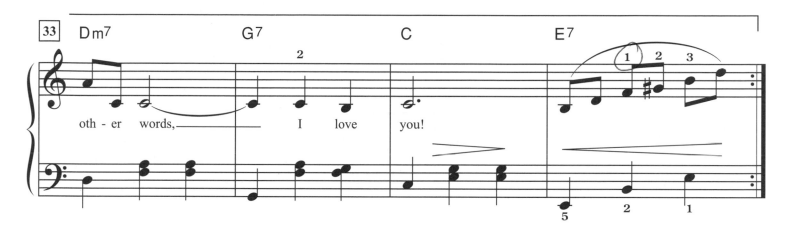

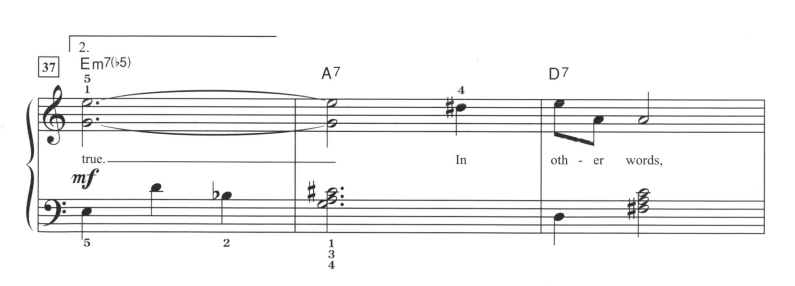

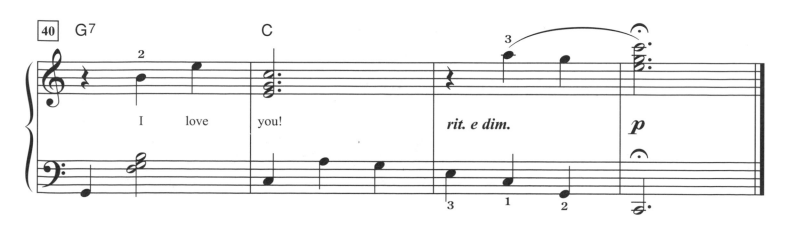

ENDLESSLY

R & B singer Brooke Benton had two hits in 1959: "It's Just a Matter of Time" (on page 65) and "Endlessly." Both were penned by Benton and Clyde Otis. Nat King Cole was originally going to record the songs, but when Otis became an A & R official at Mercury (the first African-American executive at a major record label), he persuaded Benton to sign with Mercury and record them himself.

Words and Music by Clyde Otis and Brook Benton
Arranged by Dan Coates

Moderately, with a steady beat

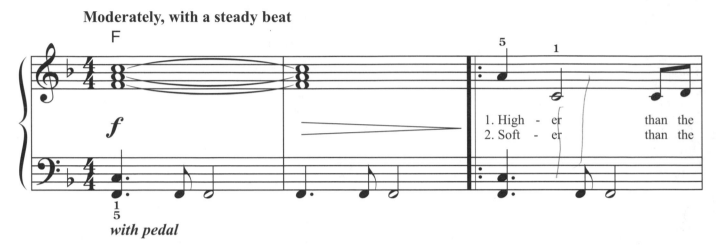

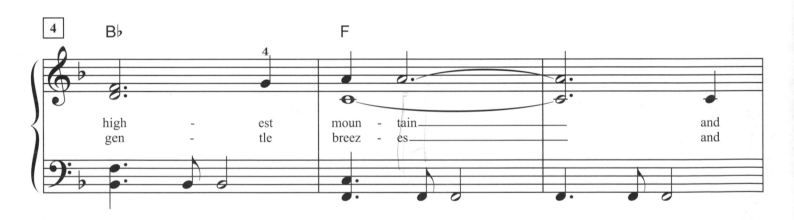

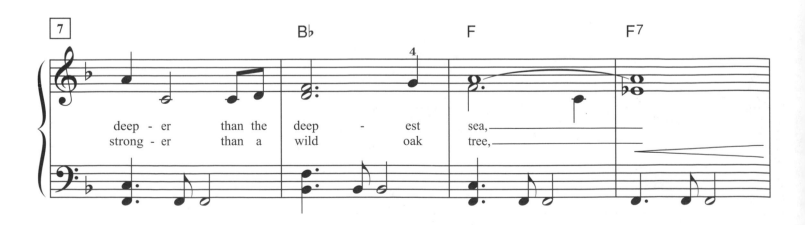

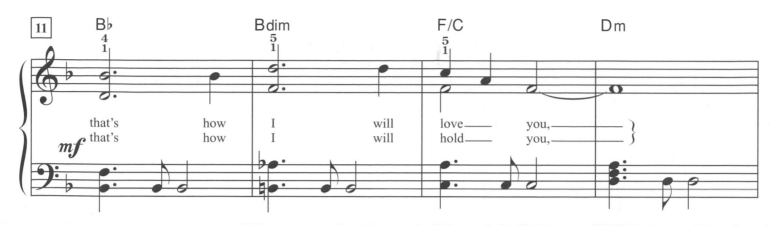

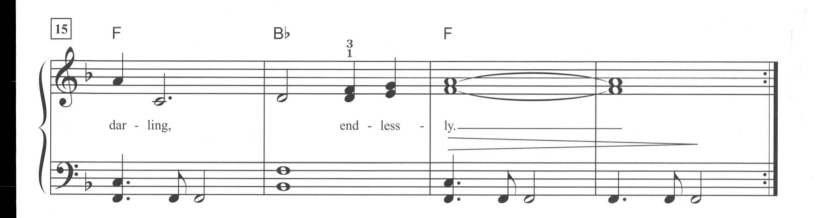

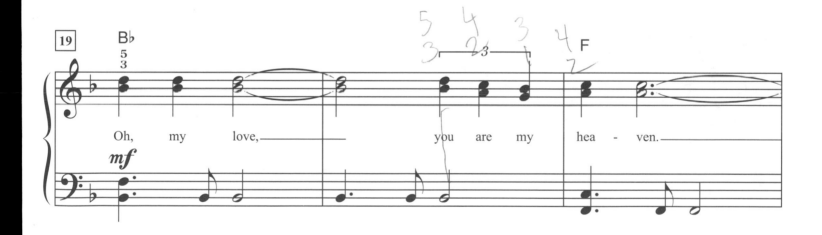

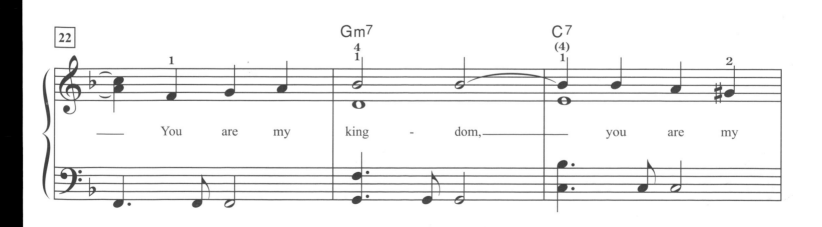

crown.   Oh,   my   love,

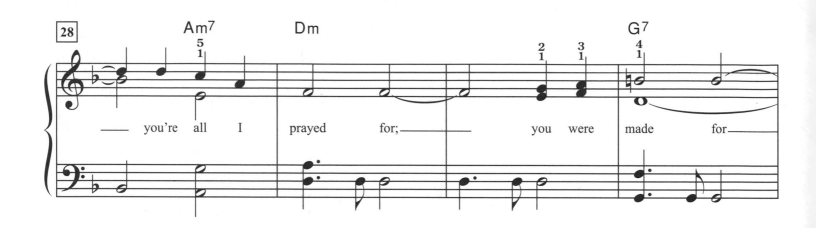

you're all I prayed   for;   you were made for

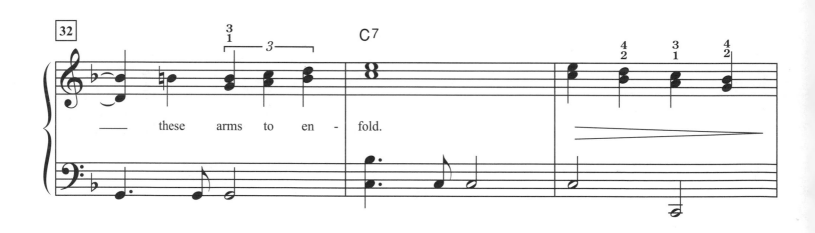

these arms to en - fold.

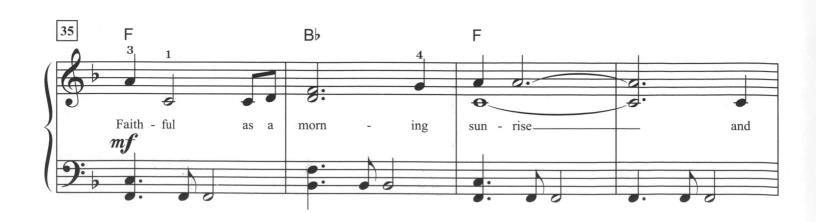

Faith - ful   as a morn - ing   sun - rise   and

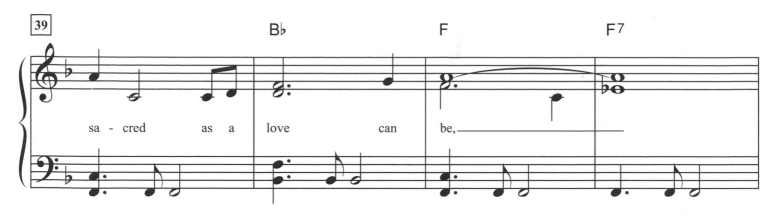

sa - cred as a love can be,_____

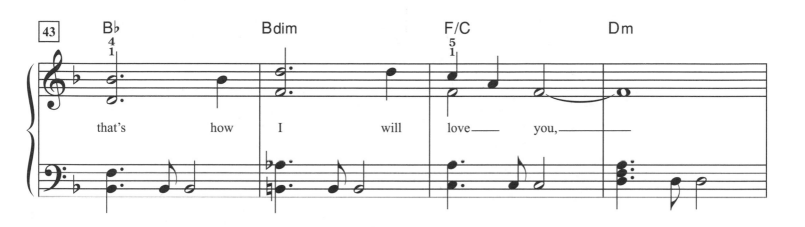

that's how I will love_____ you,_____

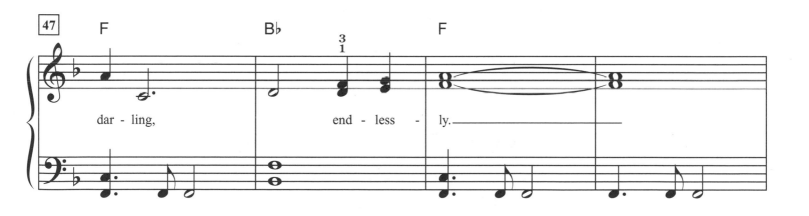

dar - ling, end - less - ly._____

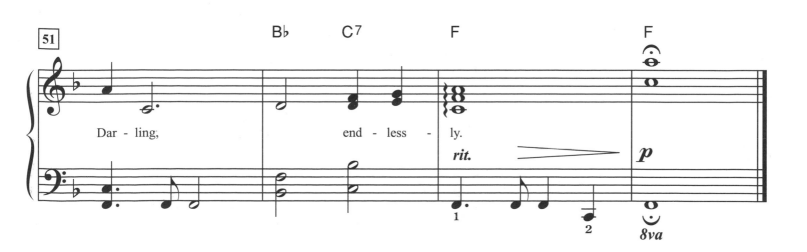

Dar - ling; end - less - ly.

rit. p

GET ME TO THE CHURCH ON TIME

"Get Me to the Church on Time" is from the 1956 musical *My Fair Lady*. It is sung by the character Alfred Doolittle towards the end of the musical. *My Fair Lady* is still a beloved part of American musical theater today, with three revivals, seven Tony Awards, and eight Academy Awards to its credit. "I Could Have Danced All Night," another popular song from the musical, is on page 54.

Lyrics by Alan Jay Lerner
Music by Frederick Loewe
Arranged by Dan Coates

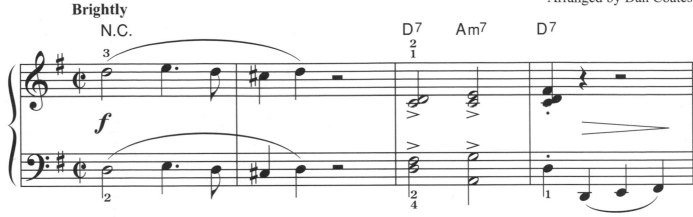

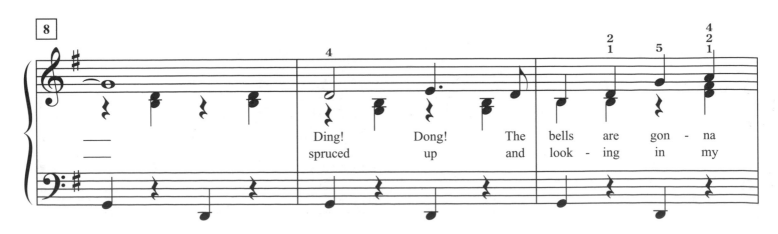

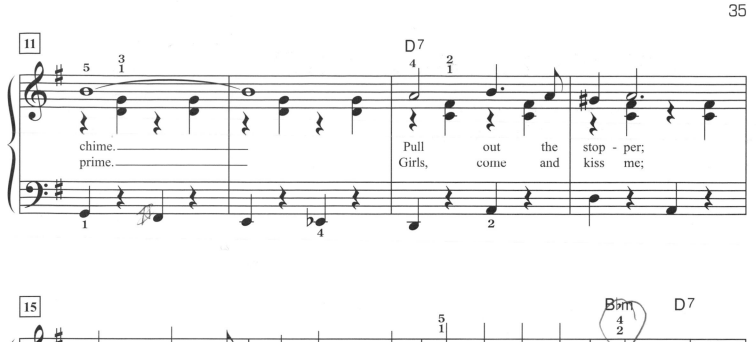

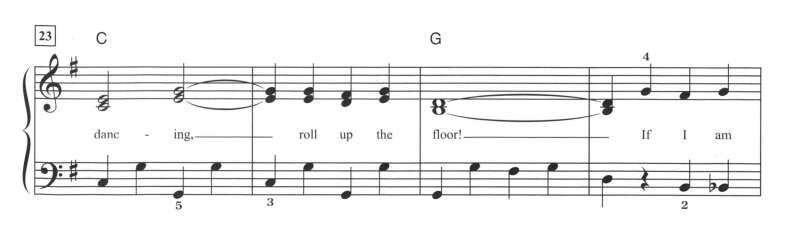

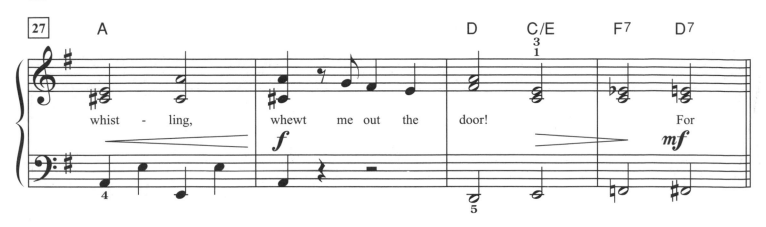

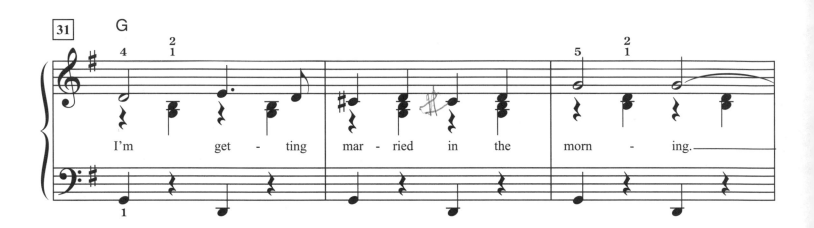

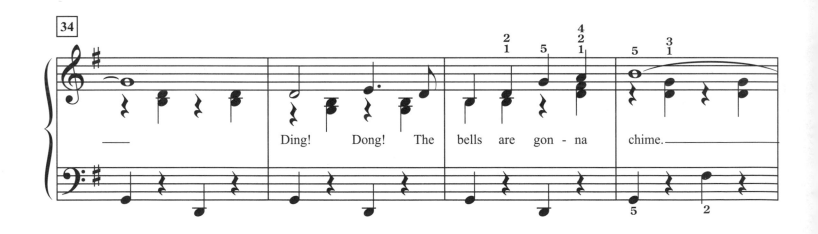

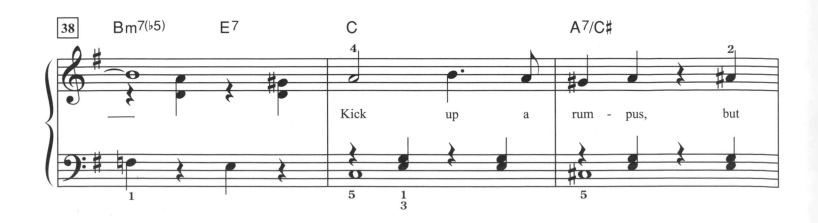

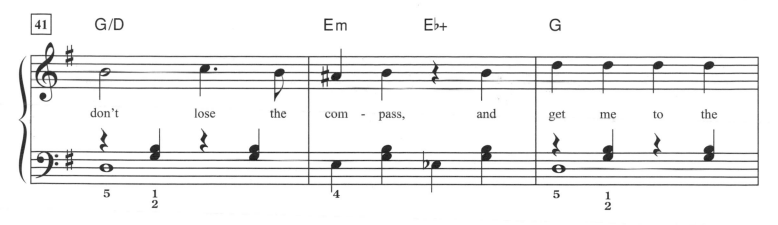

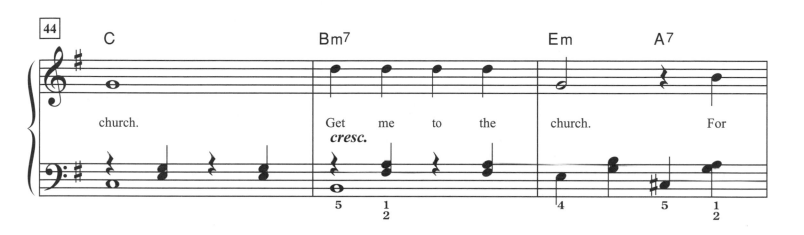

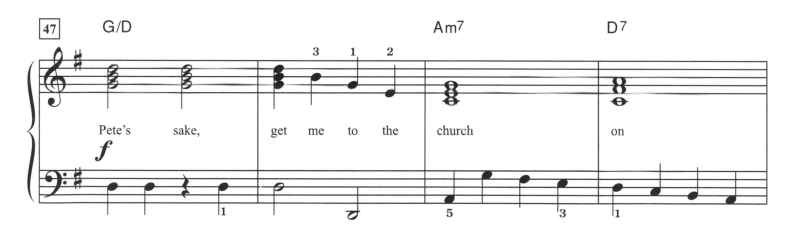

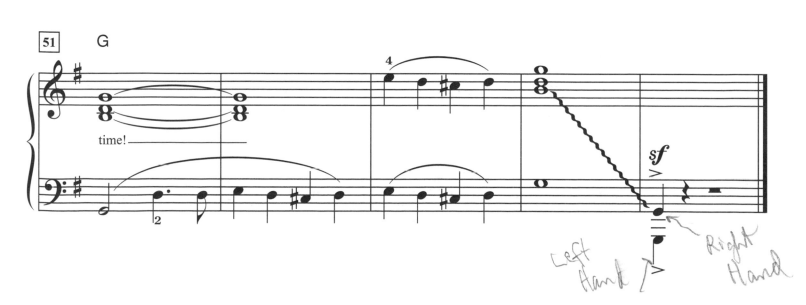

HEART

"Heart" is from the musical comedy *Damn Yankees*, which opened on Broadway in 1955. The plot is based on *Faust* but is set in 1950s Washington, D.C. "Heart" is sung by members of the Washington Senators—the jinxed baseball team which receives help from Joe Boyd, who sells his soul to the devil to become the "long ball hitter the Senators need." Richard Adler and Jerry Ross, the writers of *Damn Yankees*, also collaborated on the Broadway hit *The Pajama Game*. Sadly, Jerry Ross died just months after *Damn Yankees* opened.

Words and Music by Richard Adler and Jerry Ross
Arranged by Dan Coates

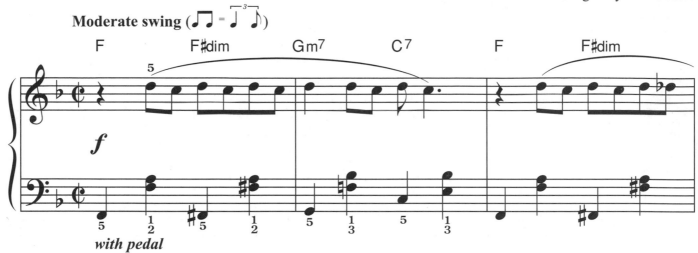

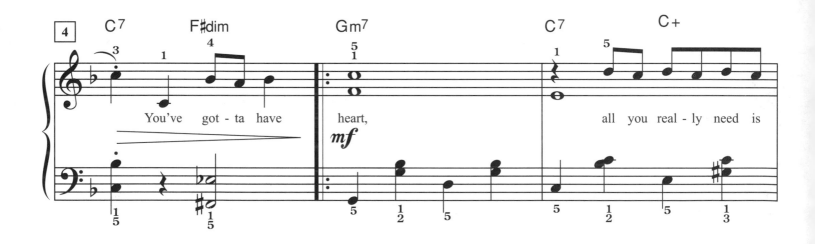

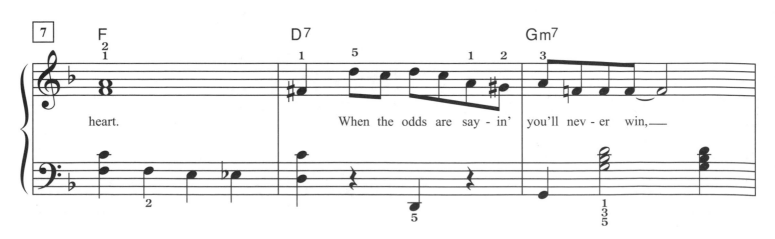

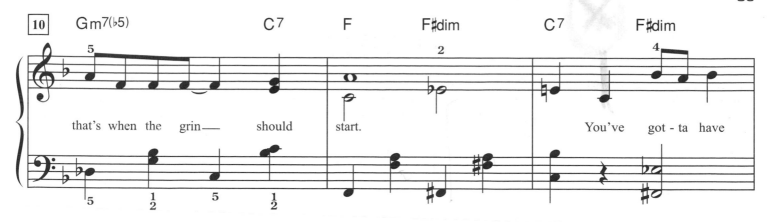

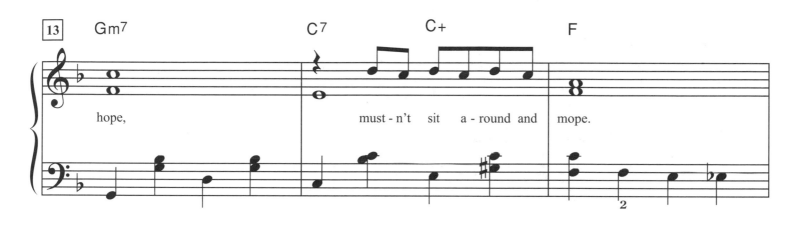

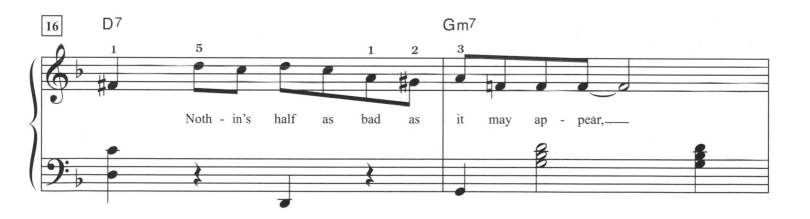

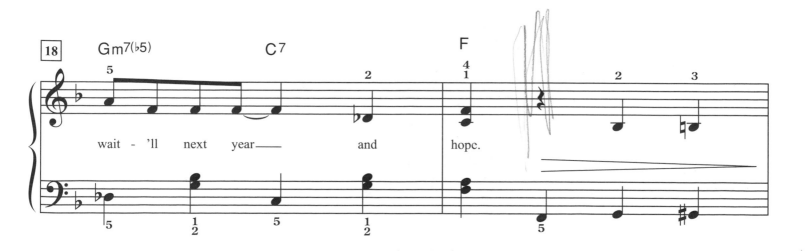

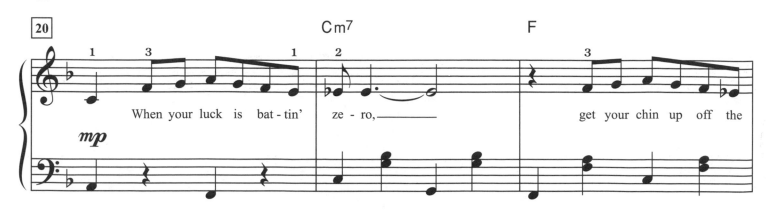

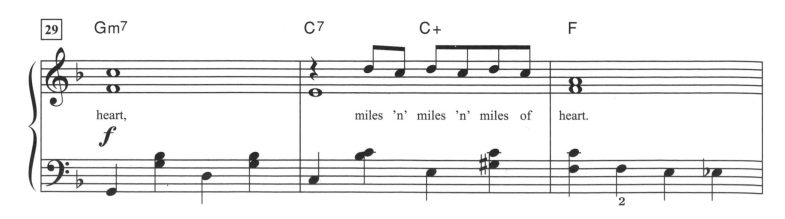

HEY THERE

"Hey There" is from the musical *The Pajama Game*, first published in 1954. The original Broadway production is credited with kick-starting the career of Shirley MacLaine. Director and producer Hal B. Wallis was an audience member at one of MacLaine's performances and signed her to Paramount Pictures. Rosemary Clooney and Sammy Davis Jr. both had #1 hits on the pop charts with their versions of "Hey There." The 2006 revival of *The Pajama Game* starred Harry Connick Jr.

Words and Music by Richard Adler and Jerry Ross
Arranged by Dan Coates

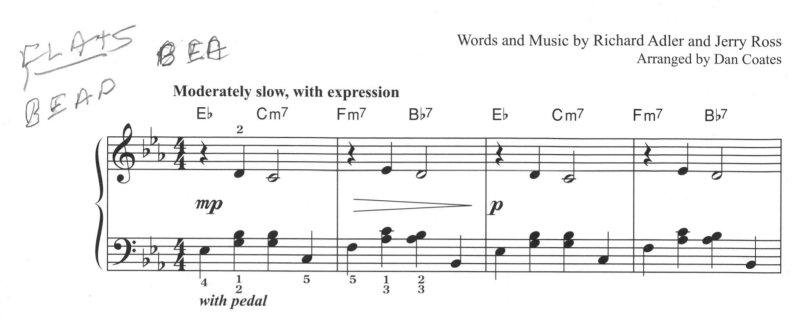

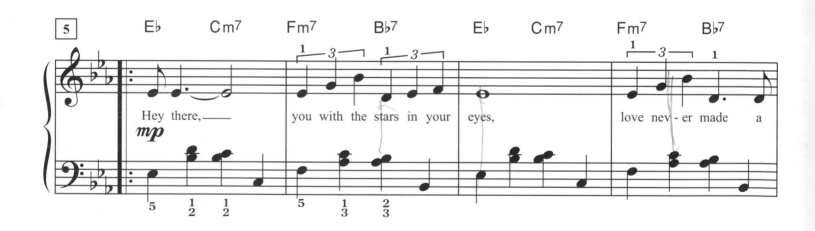

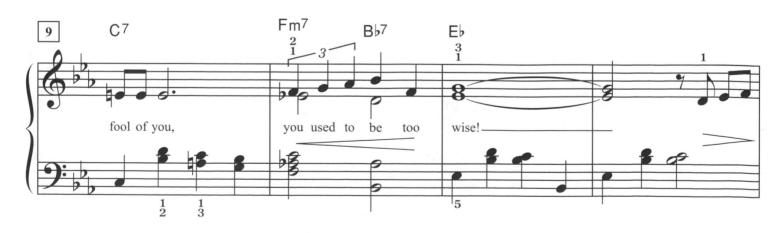

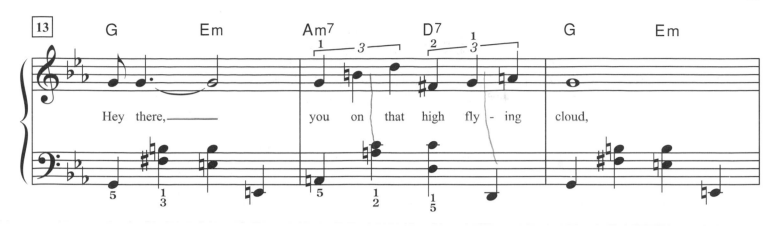

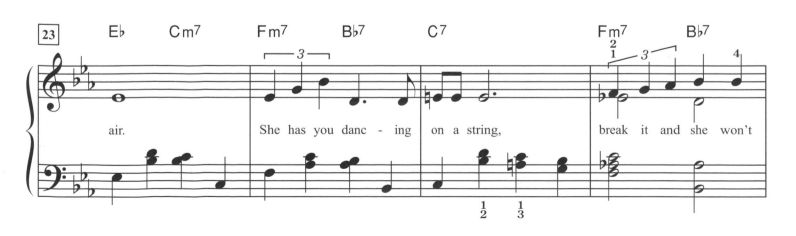

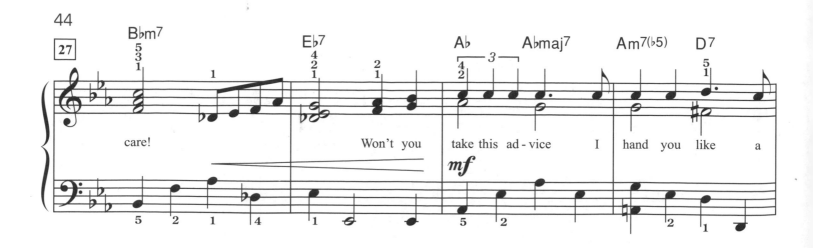

care! Won't you take this ad - vice I hand you like a

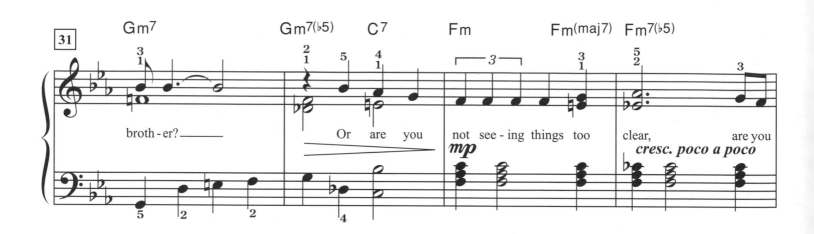

broth - er? Or are you not see - ing things too clear, are you

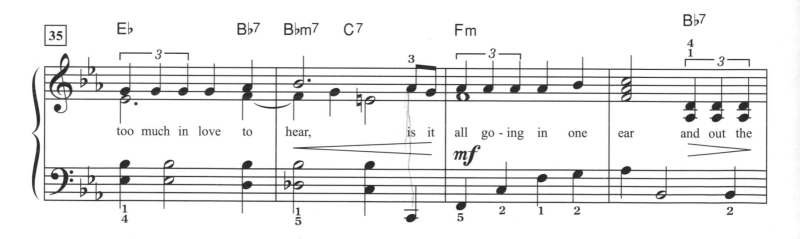

too much in love to hear, is it all go - ing in one ear and out the

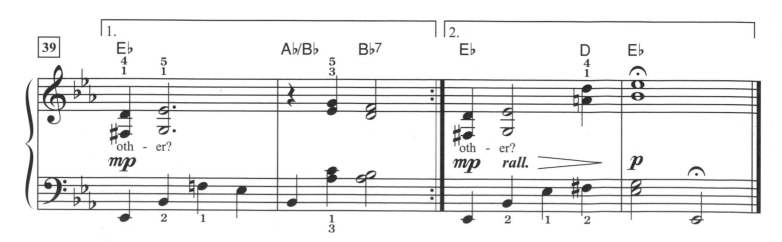

oth - er? oth - er?

HIGH NOON
(DO NOT FORSAKE ME, OH MY DARLIN')

"High Noon" is from the 1952 western film of the same name which tells the story of a town marshal who takes on a gang of killers by himself. The movie won Academy Awards for Best Actor, Film Editing, Scoring of a Dramatic or Comedy Picture, and Best Music in the song category. The song was sung in the film by Tex Ritter, father of the late actor, John Ritter.

Words by Ned Washington
Music by Dimitri Tiomkin
Arranged by Dan Coates

Moderately slow

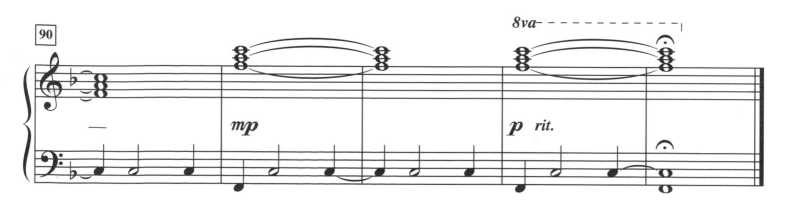

HOLD ME, THRILL ME, KISS ME

"Hold Me, Thrill Me, Kiss Me" was a hit pop song in two decades. The original version, recorded by Karen Chandler, stayed on the pop charts for 18 weeks in October of 1952. In 1965, the recording by Mel Carter, which is also the version that is more often heard, peaked at #8. Most recently, Clay Aiken sang the classic when he was a contestant on American Idol.

Words and Music by Harry Noble
Arranged by Dan Coates

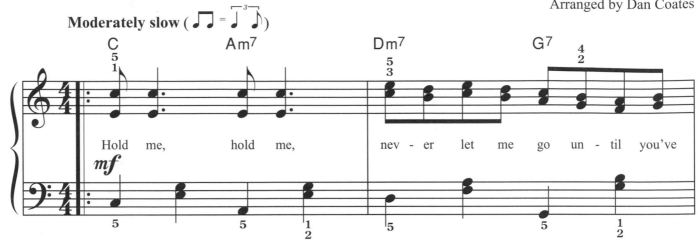

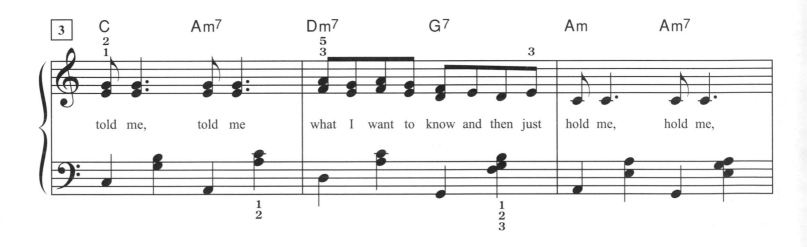

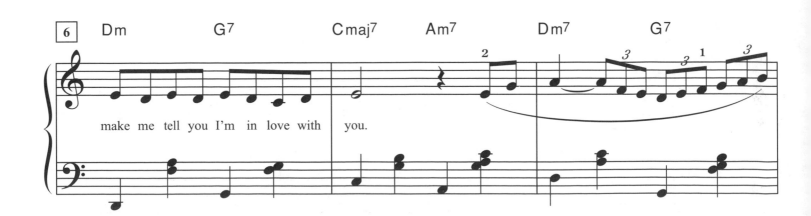

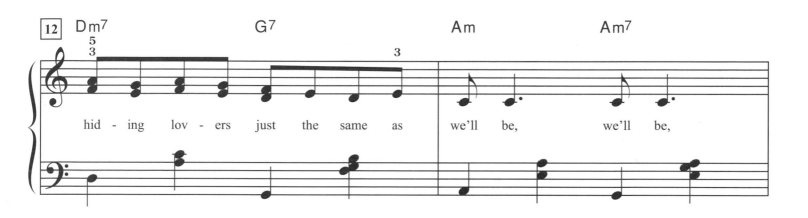

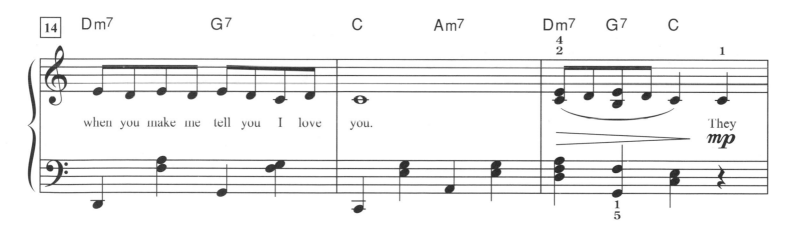

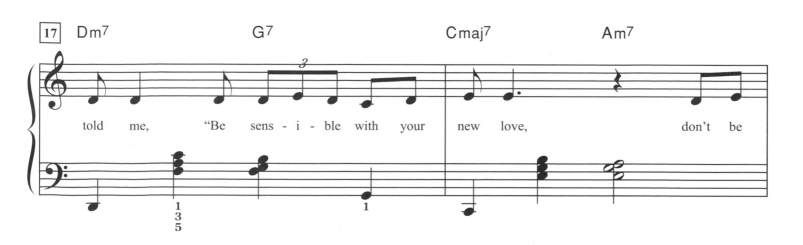

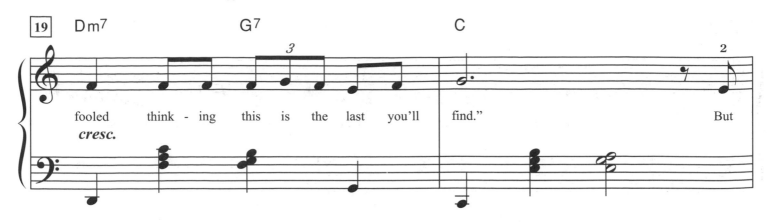

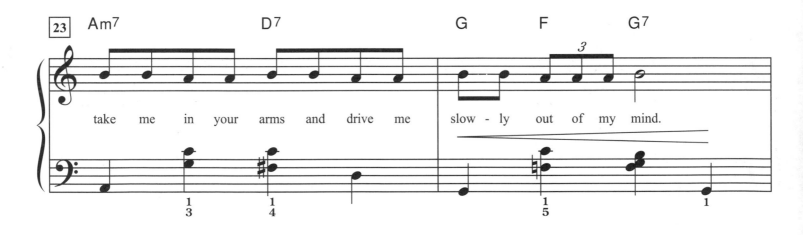

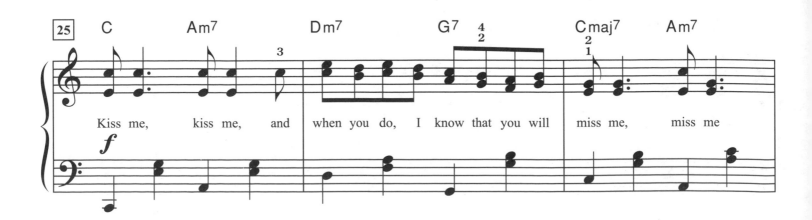

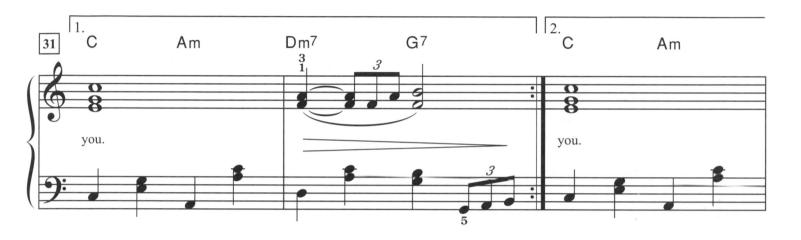

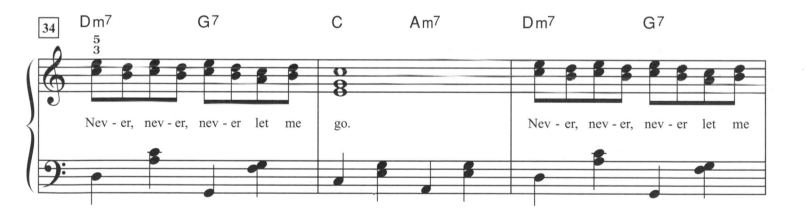

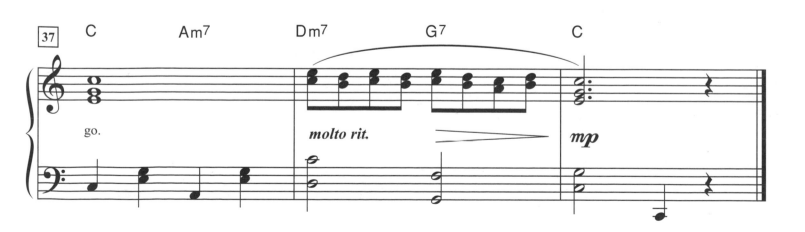

5/13/10

I COULD HAVE DANCED ALL NIGHT

"I Could Have Danced All Night" was first performed by Julie Andrews (in the role of Eliza Doolittle) in the original Broadway production of *My Fair Lady*. Doolittle is moved to sing after an unexpected dance with her tutor, Henry Higgins. In the 1964 film, Audrey Hepburn played the role of Doolittle, but the song was sung by Marni Nixon and dubbed into the film.

Lyrics by Alan Jay Lerner
Music by Frederick Loewe
Arranged by Dan Coates

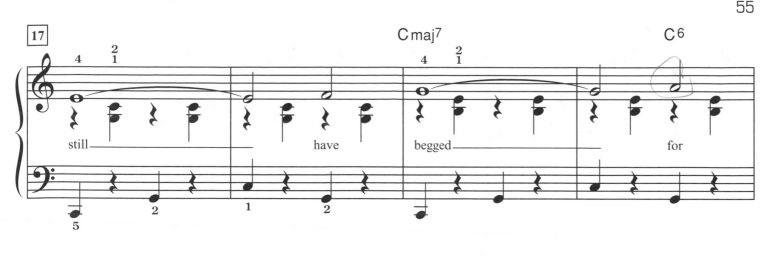

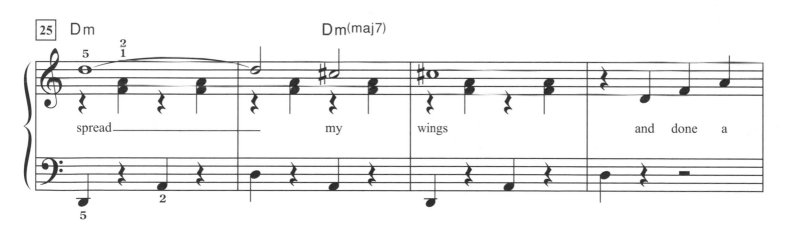

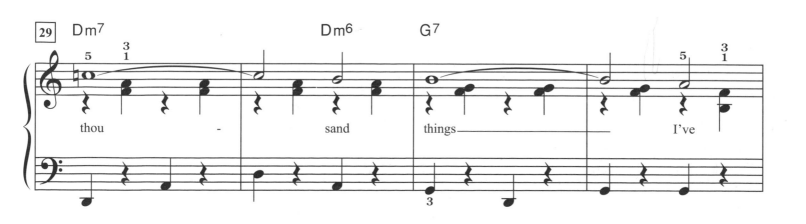

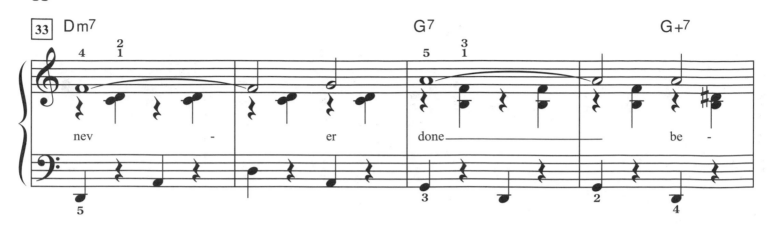

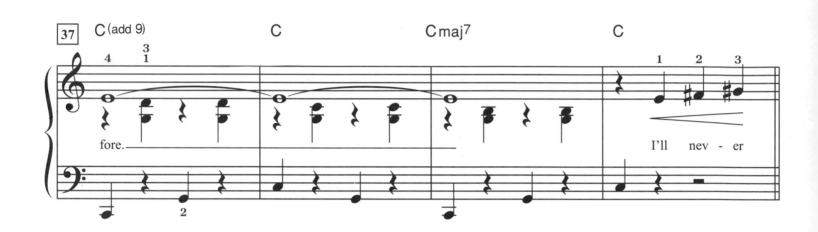

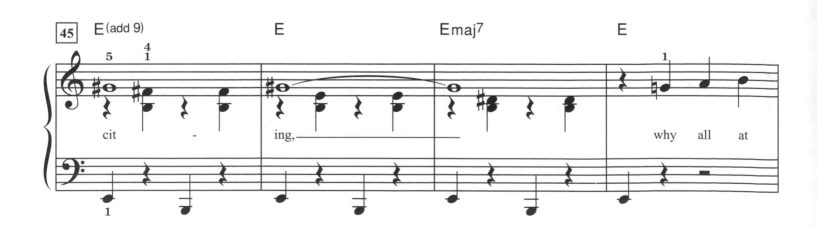

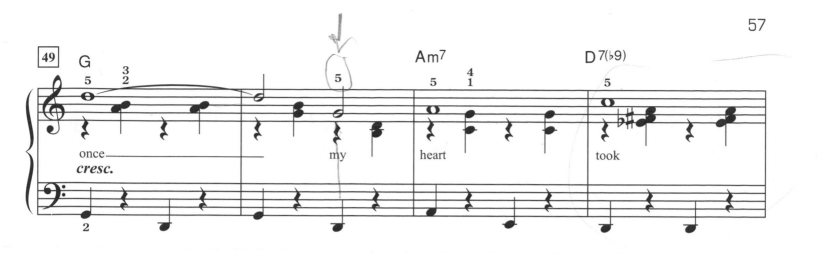

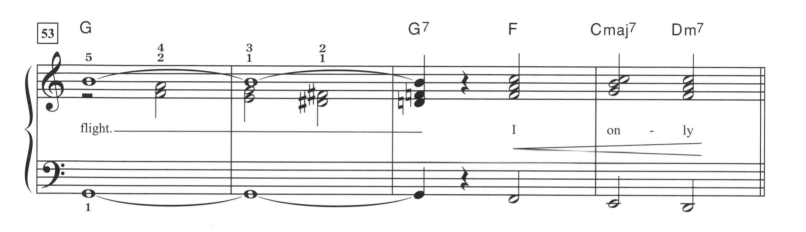

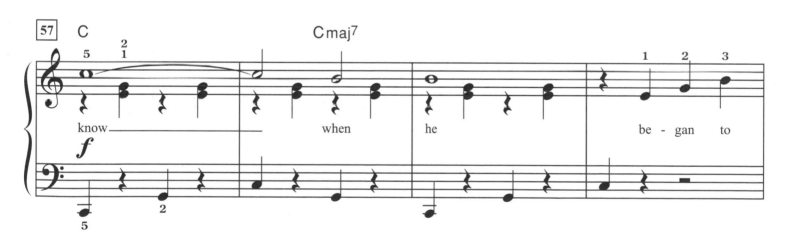

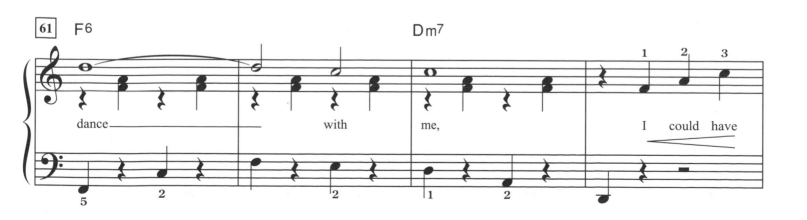

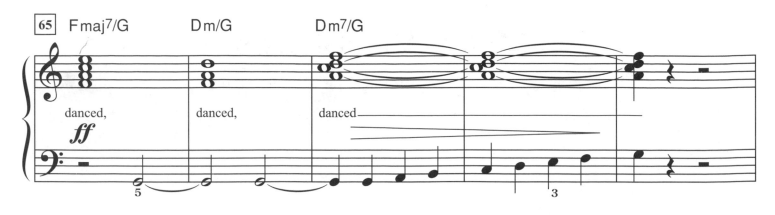

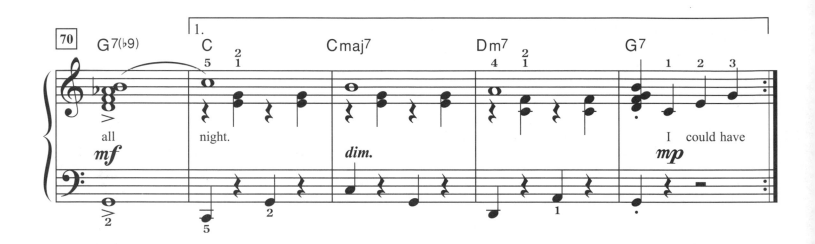

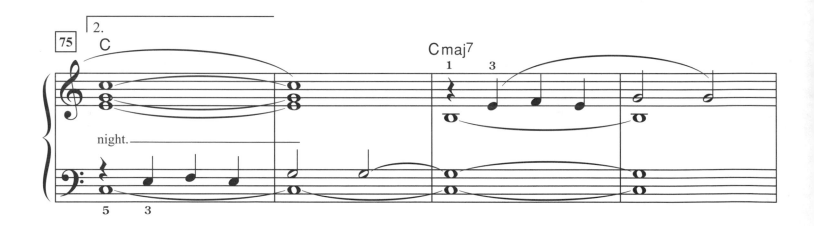

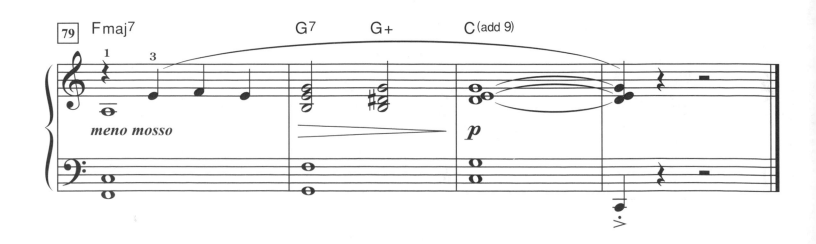

I WANNA BE AROUND

In 1958, a letter addressed to "Johnny Mercer, Songwriter; New York, NY" found its way to the lyricist. It was from an Ohio housewife named Sadie Vimmerstedt who had an idea for a song titled "When Someone Breaks Your Heart, I Want to Be Around to Pick Up the Pieces." Mercer received the letter and published the song in 1959. The 1963 Tony Bennett recording sold 15,000 copies on the first issue. Vimmerstedt is credited on the song and Mercer saw to it that she received 50 percent of the royalties.

Words and Music by
Johnny Mercer and Sadie Vimmerstedt
Arranged by Dan Coates

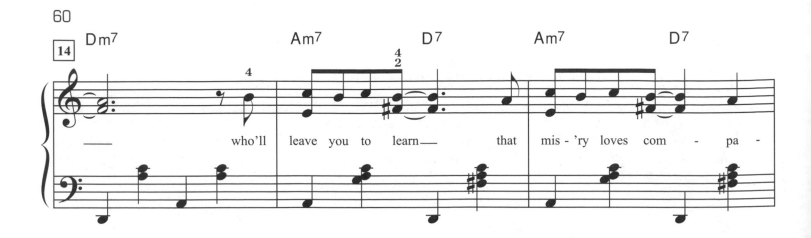

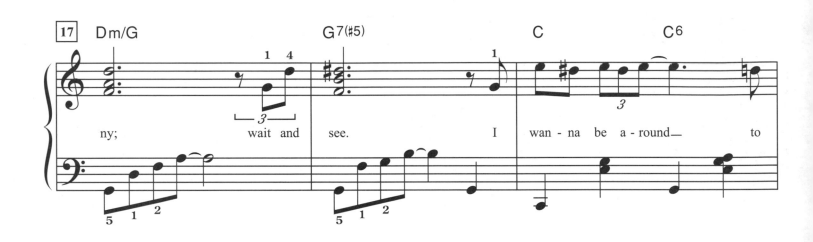

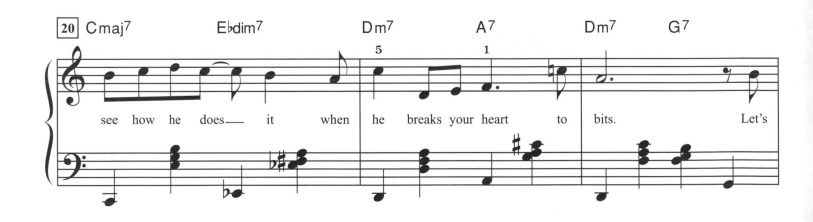

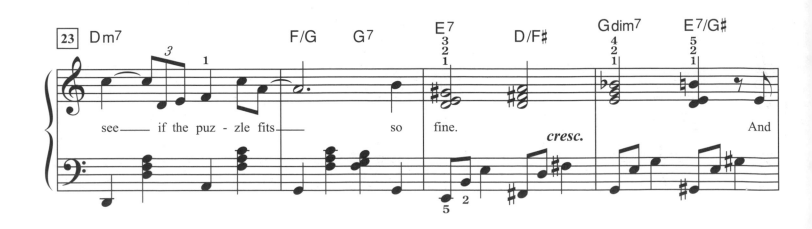

that's when I'll dis-cov-er that re - venge is sweet—— as I sit there ap-plaud-ing from a

front row seat,—— when some-bod - y breaks your heart like you broke

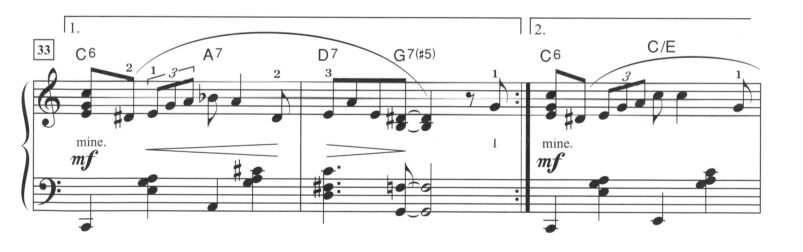

mine.

mine.

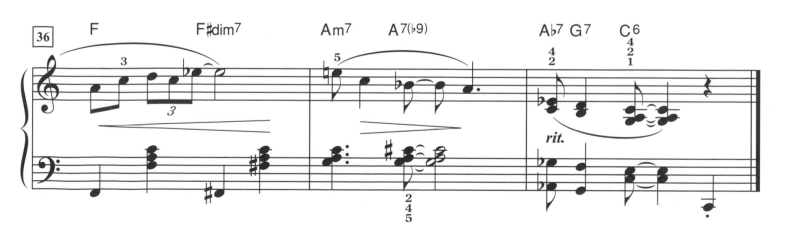

I'M WALKIN'

"I'm Walkin'" is most-associated with singer, songwriter, and pianist Fats Domino. Domino was one of the first African-American artists to cross over from R & B to the mainstream pop music market. His unique style combined blues, stride, boogie-woogie, and rock and roll. Some of his other hits include "Ain't That a Shame" and "Blueberry Hill" (on page 12). The latter was his biggest hit, which stayed at #1 on the R & B charts for 11 weeks.

Words and Music by
Antoine Domino and Dave Bartholomew
Arranged by Dan Coates

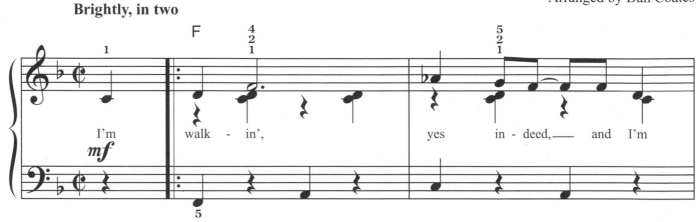

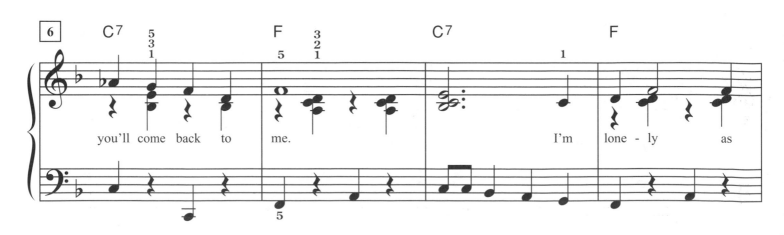

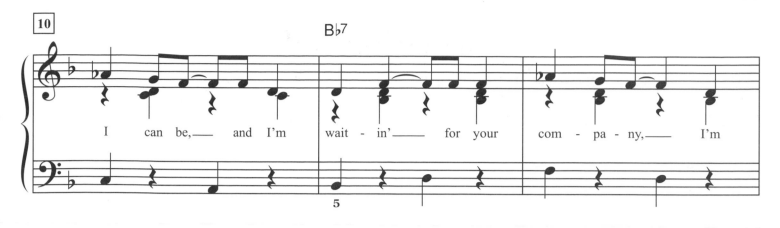

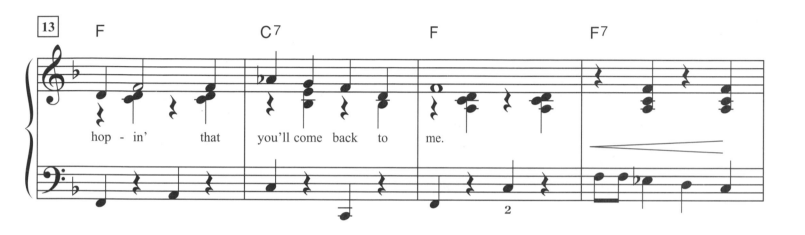

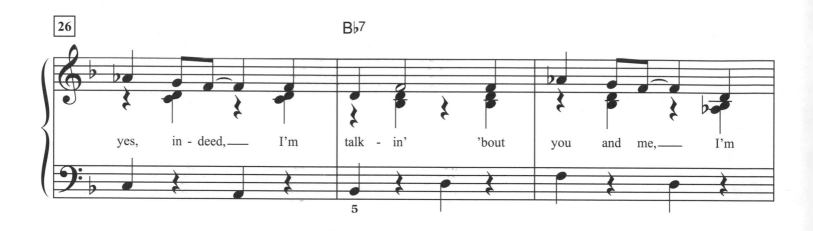

IT'S JUST A MATTER OF TIME

"It's Just a Matter of Time" was R & B singer Brook Benton's second hit from 1959. The other, "Endlessly," is on page 30. While Benton had a string of hits in the 1950s, '60s and '70s, the song he is most-known for is "Rainy Night in Georgia" which hit #1 on the charts in 1970. Benton also wrote and produced several hits for Nat King Cole, Clyde McPhatter, and Roy Hamilton.

Words and Music by
Clyde Otis, Brook Benton and Belford Hendricks
Arranged by Dan Coates

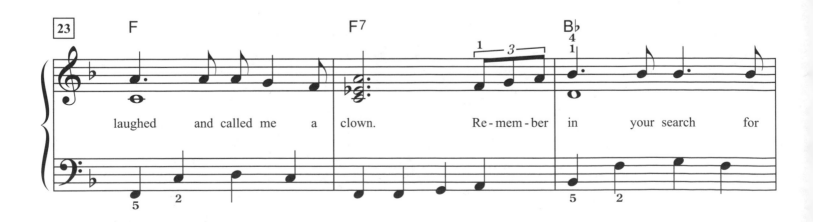

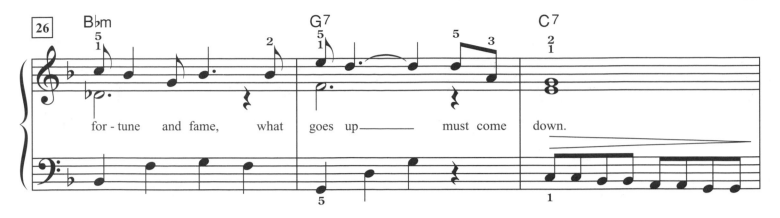

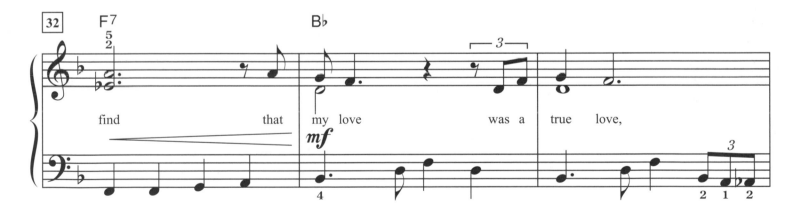

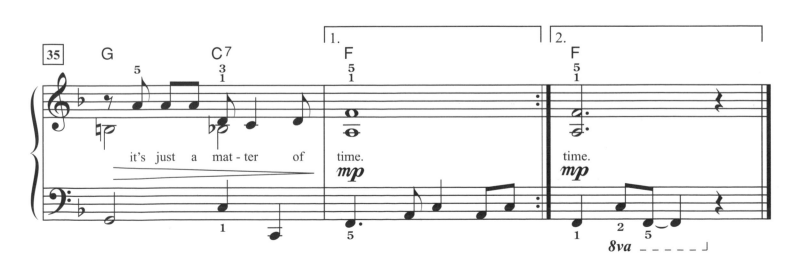

JUST IN TIME

"Just in Time" first appeared in the 1956 musical *Bells Are Ringing*, which went on to win two out of its four Emmy nominations (for Best Actress and Best Actor). More recently, "Just in Time" was featured on the 2006 Tony Bennett album *Duets: An American Classic* on which the iconic singer sang a duet with Michael Bublé.

Lyrics by Betty Comden and Adolph Green
Music by Jule Styne
Arranged by Dan Coates

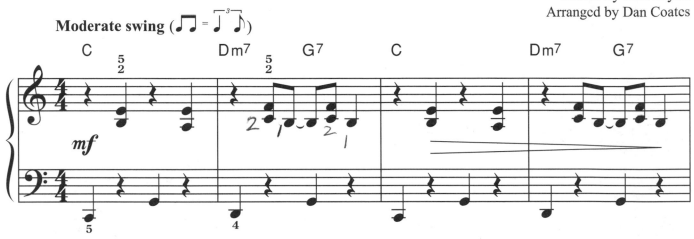

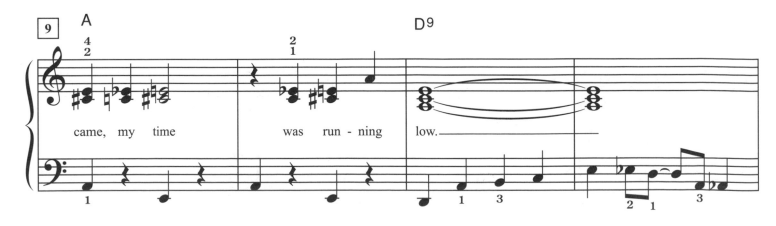

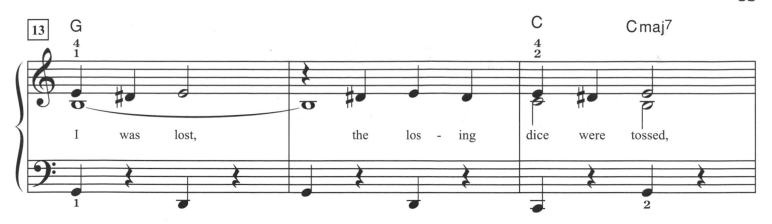

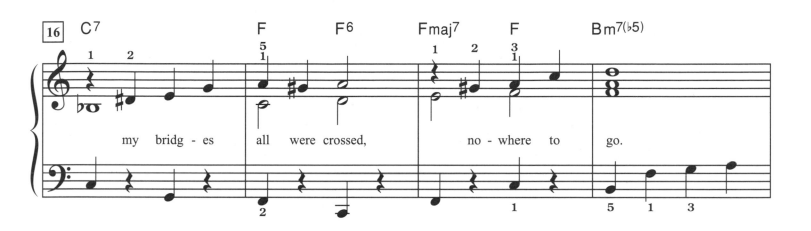

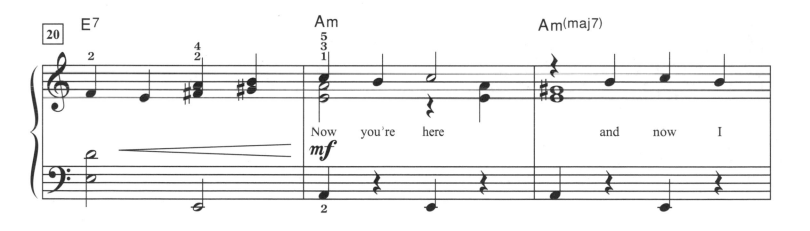

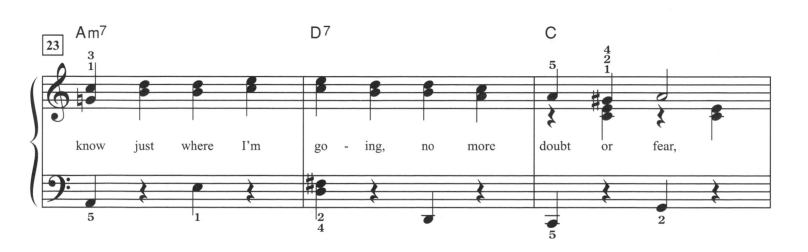

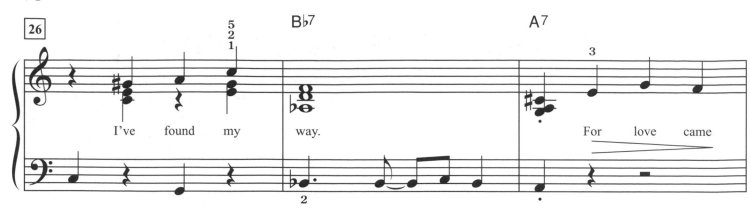

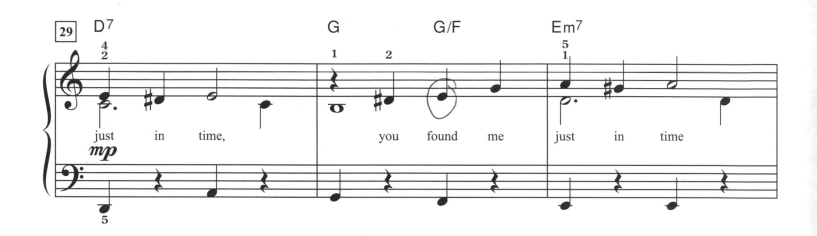

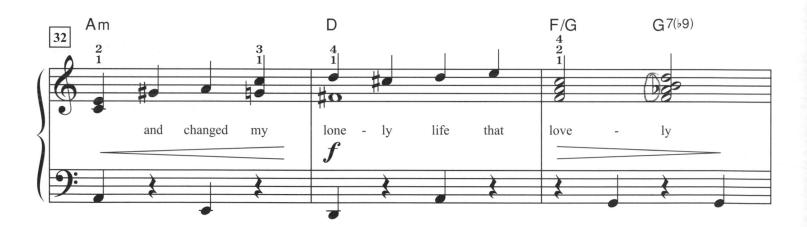

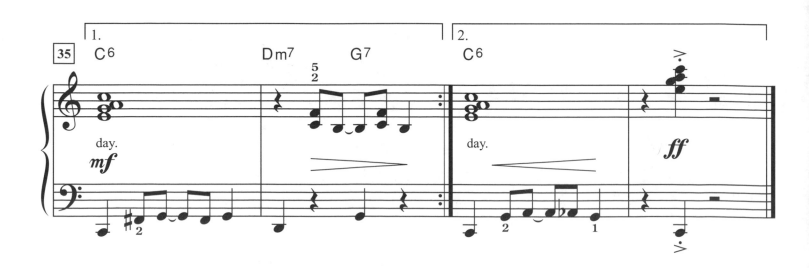

LET THE GOOD TIMES ROLL

The most well-known version of "Let the Good Times Roll" is from 1956 and features the duo Shirley and Lee (Shirley Goodman and Leonard Lee) who also penned the tune. This hit is loosely based on the 1946 song of the same name which was performed by Louis Jordan. Since 1956, "Let the Good Times Roll" has been covered by a wide array of artists including: Barbra Streisand, Harry Nilsson, Ike & Tina Turner, The Righteous Brothers, B. B. King, Roy Orbison, and many more.

Words and Music by
Leonard Lee and Shirley Goodman
Arranged by Dan Coates

1. Come on, ba - by, let the good times roll,___
2. Come on, ba - by, gon - na have a ball,___

come on, ba - by, let me thrill your soul.___
put our trou - bles up a - gainst the wall.___

Come on, ba - by, let the

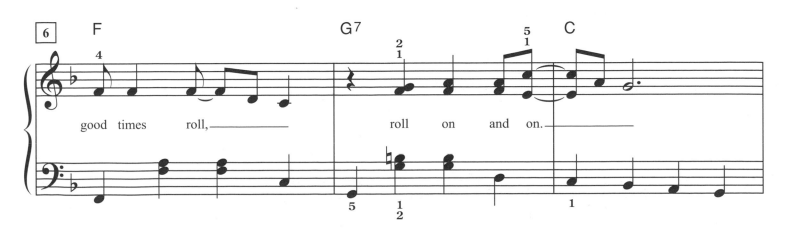

good times roll,___ roll on and on.___

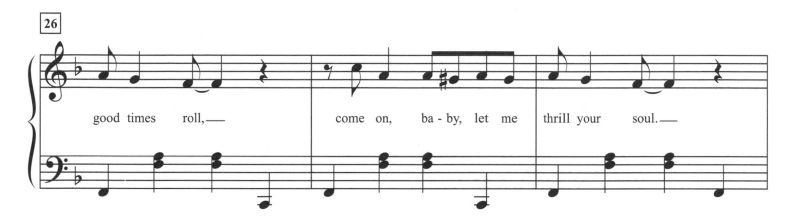

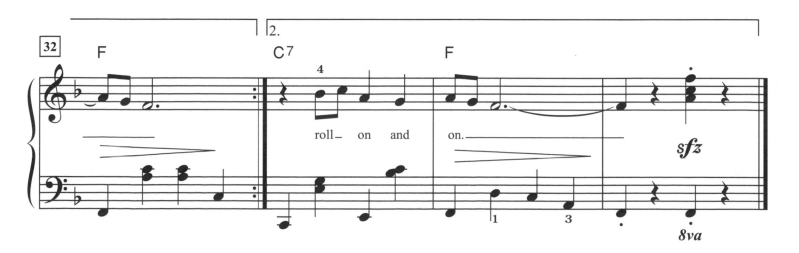

LOVE IS A MANY SPLENDORED THING

This classic song was featured in the 1955 movie *Love Is a Many Splendored Thing*. The movie went on to win an Academy Award for Best Song. The best-selling version of the song was recorded by The Four Aces which reached #1 on the Billboard charts in 1955. "Love Is a Many Splendored Thing" has been recorded by Frank Sinatra and Andy Williams, and in 2006 Barry Manilow included the hit on his album *The Greatest Songs of the Fifties*.

Music by Sammy Fain
Lyric by Paul Francis Webster
Arranged by Dan Coates

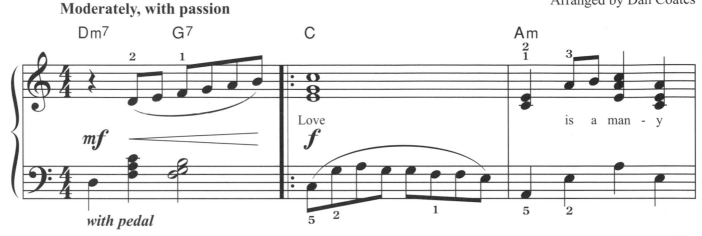

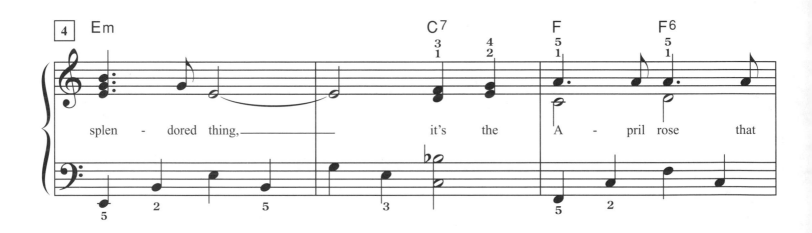

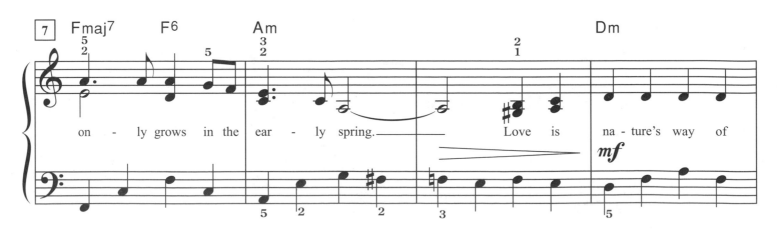

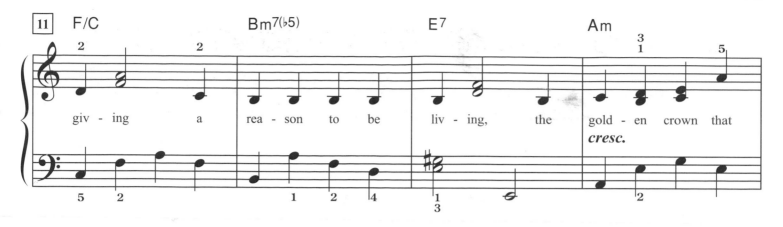

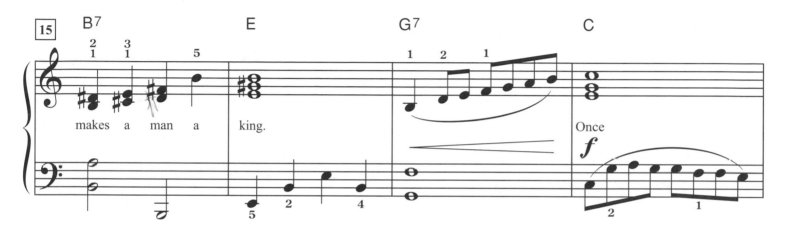

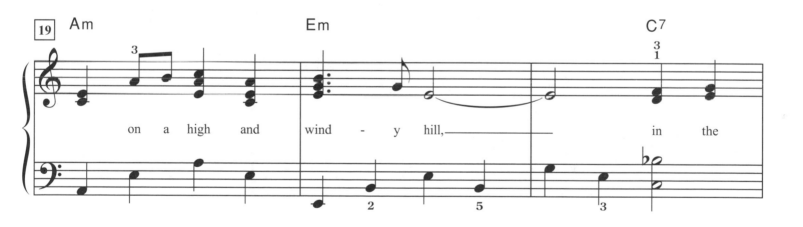

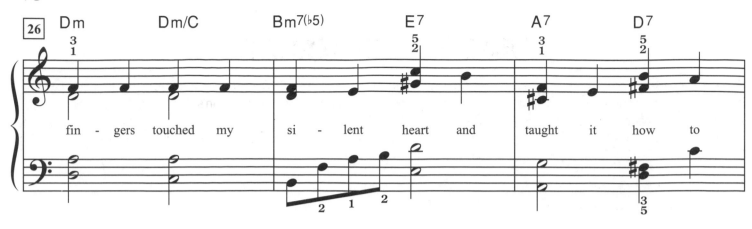

fin - gers touched my si - lent heart and taught it how to

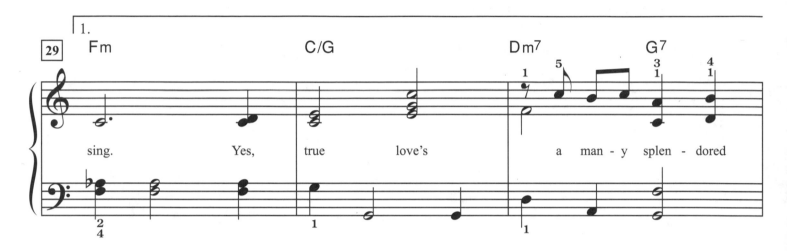

sing. Yes, true love's a man - y splen - dored

thing. sing. Yes,

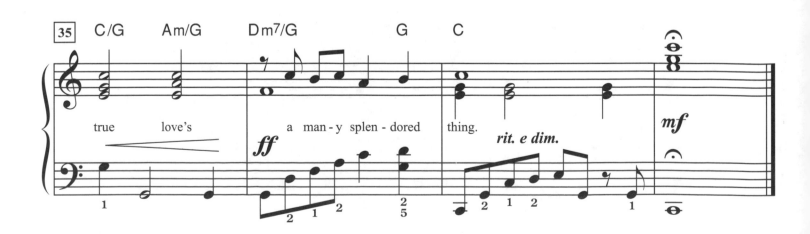

true love's a man - y splen - dored thing.

MACK THE KNIFE

"Mack the Knife" is from *The Threepenny Opera* which premiered in Berlin in 1928. It first hit the U.S. pop charts in 1954 when Louis Armstrong recorded it. However, the most well-known recording is Bobby Darin's 1958 version which reached #1 on the pop charts in 1959. Initially, Dick Clark advised Darin not to record the song because it was from an opera and would doubtfully appeal to the young, rock and roll audience. Many others have recorded the song including: Frank Sinatra, Ella Fitzgerald, Robbie Williams, Bill Haley & His Comets, and Tito Puente.

English Words by Marc Blitzstein
Original German Words by Bert Brecht

Music by Kurt Weill
Arranged by Dan Coates

MALAFEMMENA
(ANGEL WITH A DEVIL'S HEART)

This song was made famous by Concetta Rosa Maria Franconero, who later changed her name to Connie Francis. One of the most popular singers of the 1950s, Connie Francis released numerous recordings of Italian songs when other singers feared that showcasing their Italian heritage would hurt their careers. The opposite was true, and Francis' success paved the way for an insurgence of Italian songs including "Arrivederci Roma" (on page 4), "Cara Mia" (on page 15), "Non Dimenticar" (on page 86), "Volare" (on page 134), and more.

English Words by George Brown
Italian Words and Music by Toto
Arranged by Dan Coates

Moderately, with a Tango feeling

for you just can't be true.

Yes you are _____ an an-gel who has lost her way, _____

_____ you gave your love, then let it stray, _____ know - ing I still loved

you. Half a man, _____

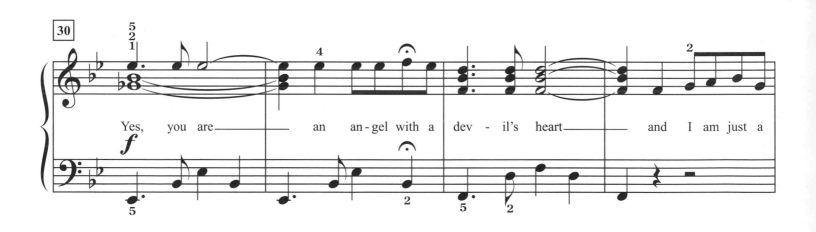

MISTY

8/11/52

"Misty" was originally composed as an instrumental jazz piece in 1954 by the legendary pianist Erroll Garner. Lyrics were later added and it went on to become one of the most recorded vocal jazz standards. Just a few of the artists who have recorded "Misty" are: Ella Fitzgerald, Frank Sinatra, Aretha Franklin, Freddie Hubbard, McCoy Tyner, Duke Ellington, Etta James, Julie London, Dave Koz, Jackie Gleason, Dexter Gordon, Johnny Mathis, Dianne Reeves, Kenny Rogers, Doc Severinsen, Sarah Vaughan, Oscar Peterson, Itzhak Perlman, Wes Montgomery, and many others.

Words by Johnny Burke
Music by Erroll Garner
Arranged by Dan Coates

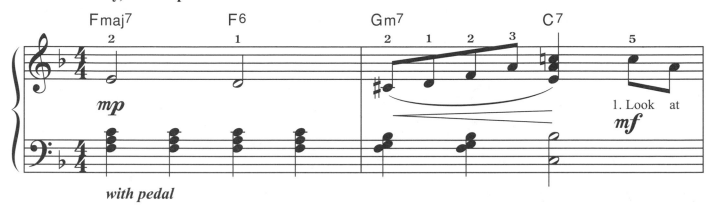

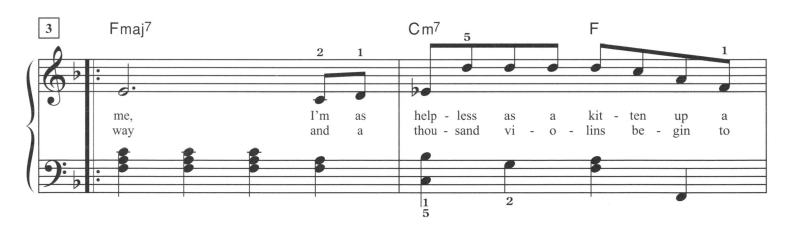

84

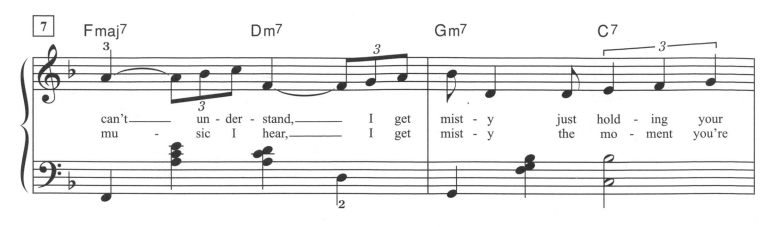

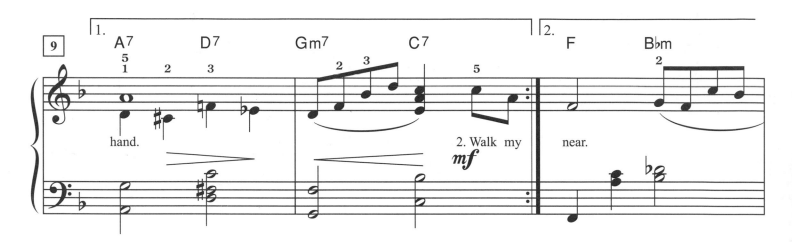

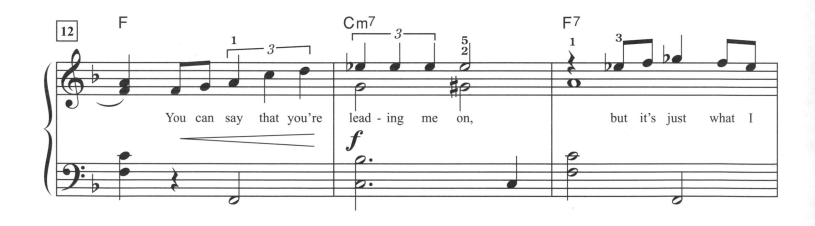

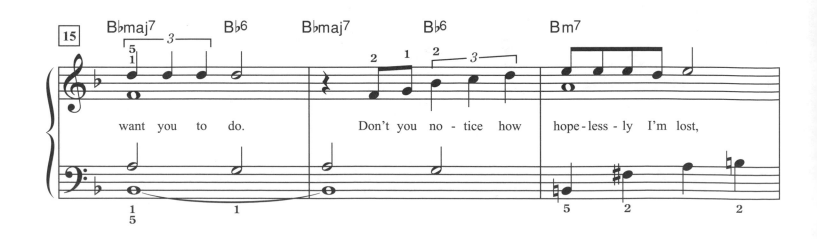

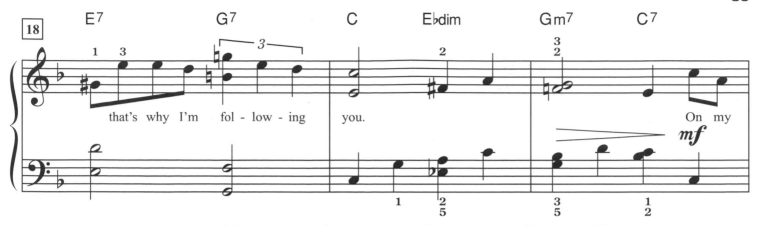

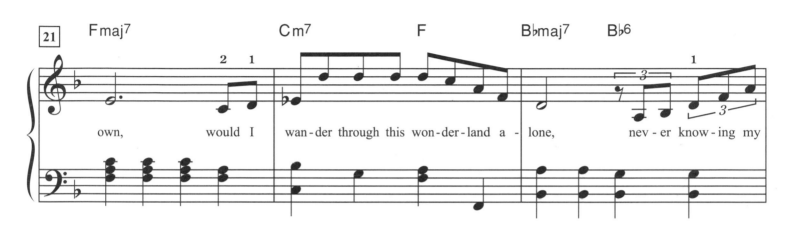

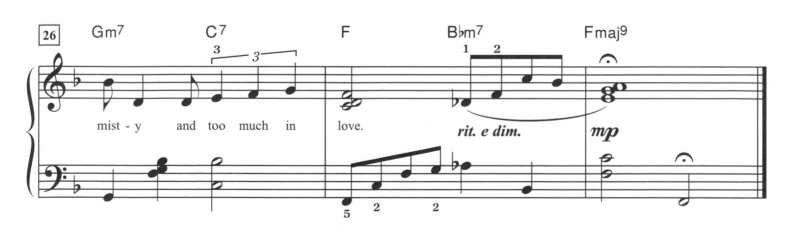

NON DIMENTICAR
(T'HO VOLUTO BENE)

"Non Dimenticar" (Italian for "Don't Forget") was featured in the 1951 Italian melodrama, *Anna*, and sung by the lead, Silvana Mangano. In the movie, Mangano plays a former night club singer who becomes a nun. While Mangano's performance was well-received, the song didn't achieve popularity until Nat King Cole recorded it in 1958. Other singers who recorded the hit include: Dean Martin, Connie Francis, Jerry Vale, Frankie Avalon, and more.

English Lyric by Shelley Dobbins
Original Italian Lyrics by Michelle Galdieri

Music by P. G. Redi
Arranged by Dan Coates

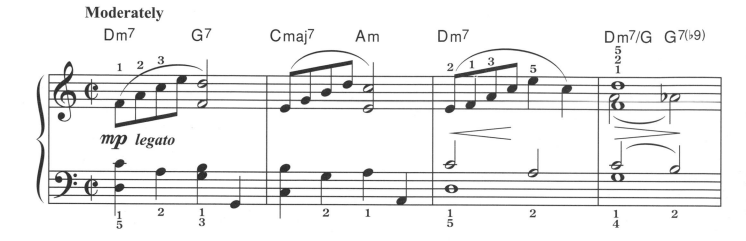

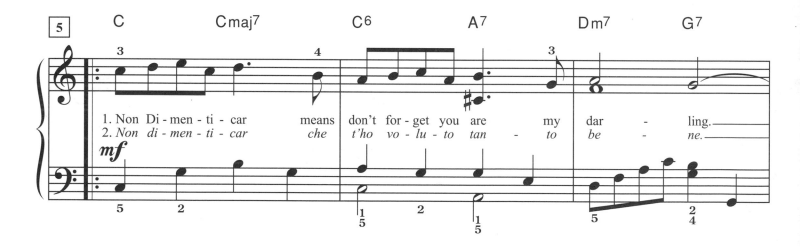

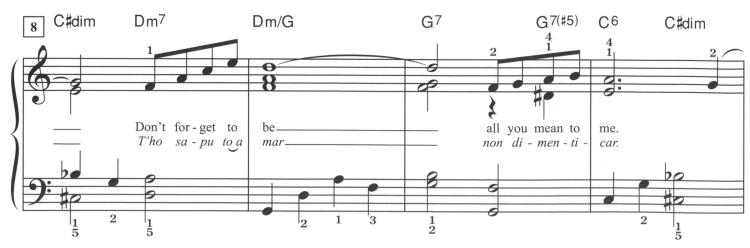

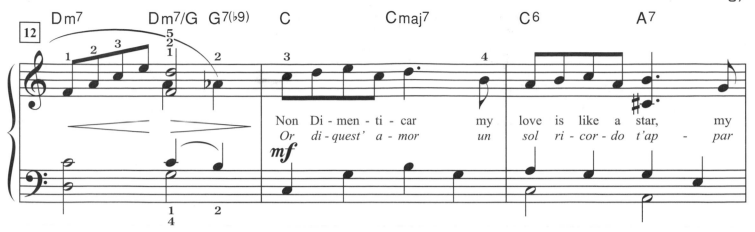

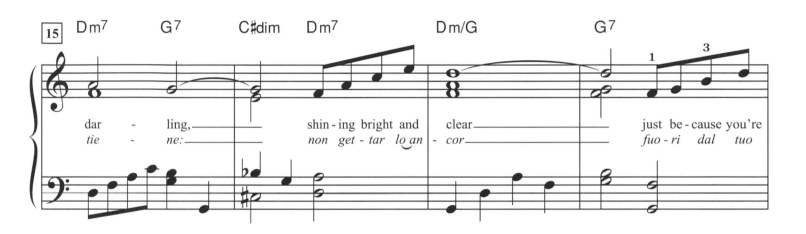

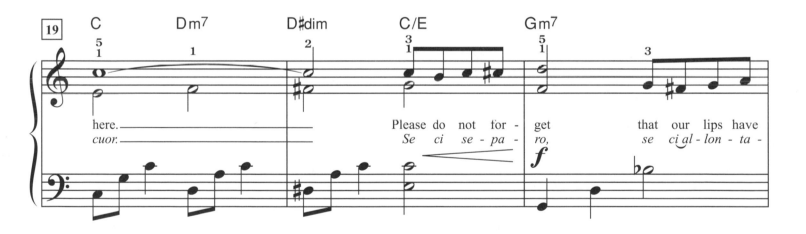

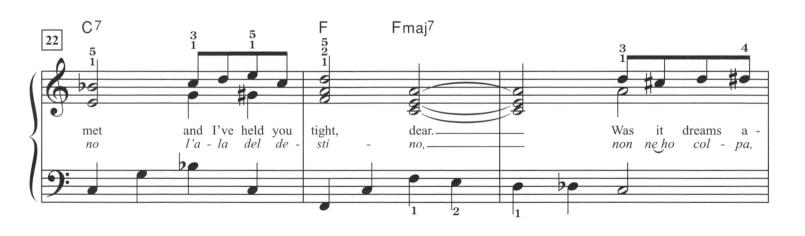

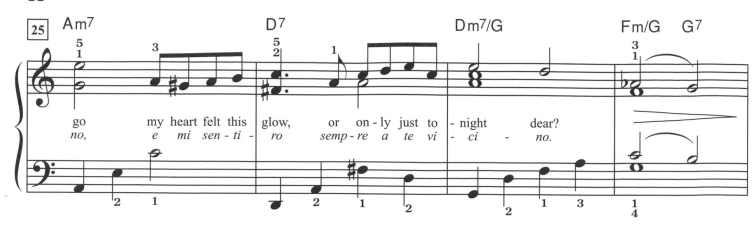

25 | Am7 ... D7 ... Dm7/G ... Fm/G G7

go, my heart felt this glow, or on - ly just to - night dear?
no, e mi sen - ti - ro semp - re a te vi - ci - no.

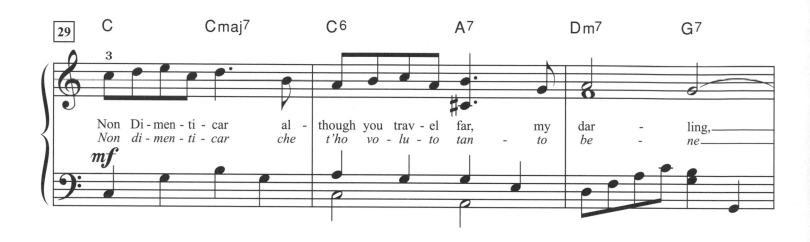

29 | C Cmaj7 C6 A7 Dm7 G7

mf

Non Di - men - ti - car al - though you trav - el far, my dar - ling,
Non di - men - ti - car che t'ho vo - lu - to tan - to be - ne

32 | C#dim Dm7 Dm7/G G7 G7(♭9)

it's my heart you own, so I'll wait a - lone, Non Di - men - ti -
For - se nel mio cuor puoi tro - va - re an - cor tan - to e tan to a-

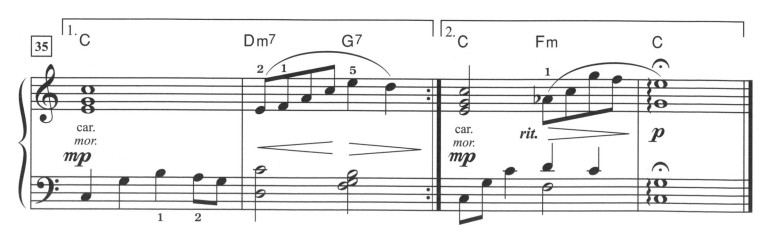

35 | 1. C Dm7 G7 | 2. C Fm C

car.
mor.
mp

car.
mor.
mp

rit.

p

RAGS TO RICHES

"Rags to Riches" was recorded by Tony Bennett in 1953 and reached #1 on the Billboard charts that same year. In 2006, Bennett recorded a duet version with Elton John for the album *Duets: An American Classic*, which debuted at #3 on the Billboard charts. It is no surprise "Rags to Riches" has had such long-term success; it was penned by the duo of Richard Adler and Jerry Ross, who collaborated on the Broadway hits *The Pajama Game* and *Damn Yankees*.

Words and Music by Richard Adler and Jerry Ross
Arranged by Dan Coates

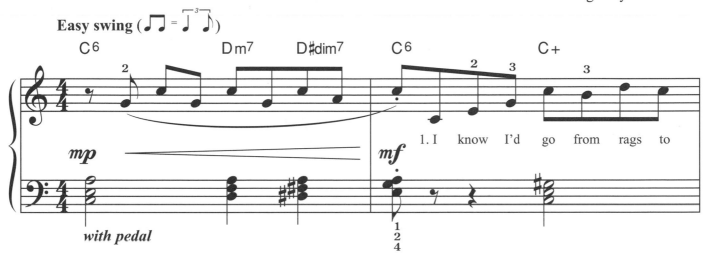

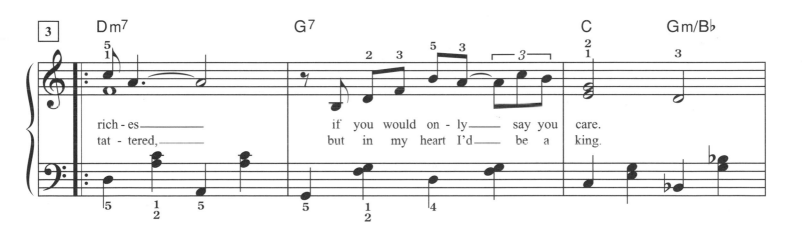

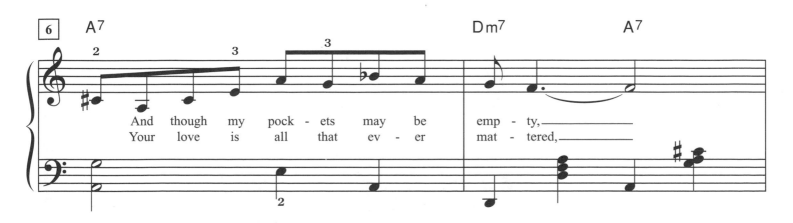

10/41/12

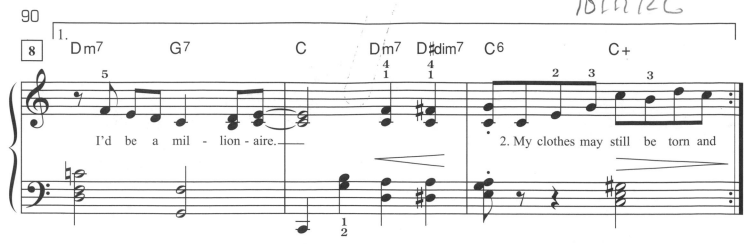

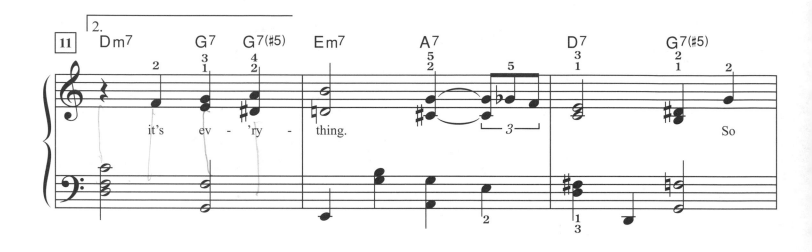

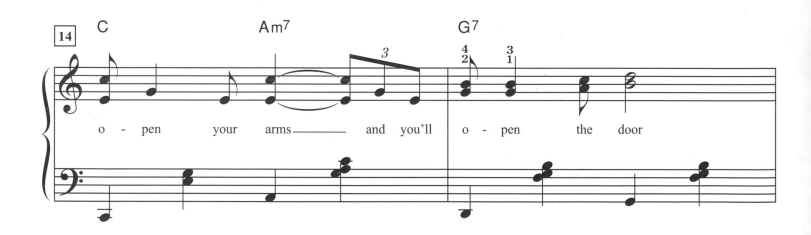

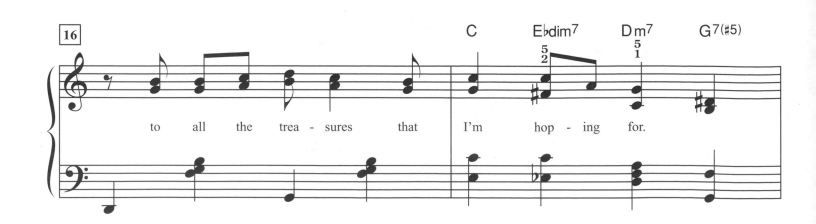

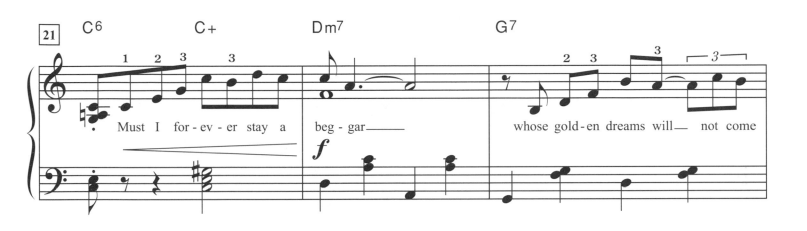

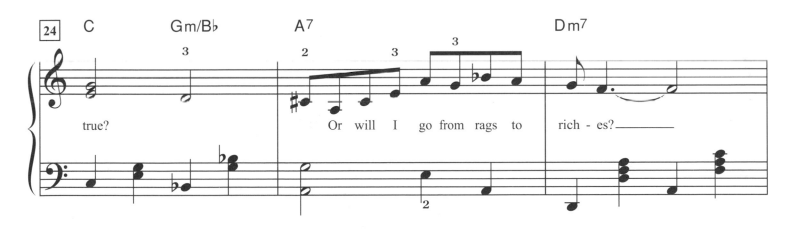

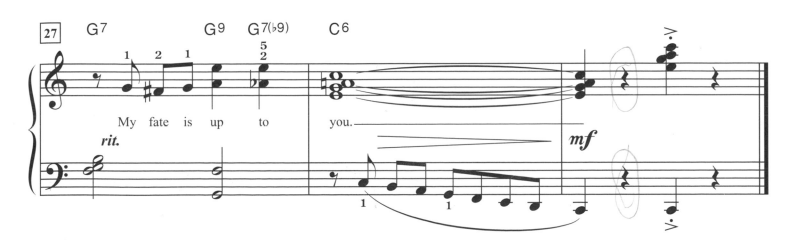

PETER GUNN

This famous theme was used at the opening and closing of the 1950s television show *Peter Gunn*. Composed by Henry Mancini, the show's usage of jazz was cutting edge. Until that time, most television shows underscored action with bland orchestral music. The catchy bass line in "Peter Gunn" has been sampled by countless artists and used in movies and television shows. Mancini won an Emmy Award and two Grammy Awards for this classic theme.

By Henry Mancini
Arranged by Dan Coates

A ROCKIN' GOOD WAY
(TO MESS AROUND AND FALL IN LOVE)

One of the most popular recordings of this tune was sung by "Queen of the Blues" Dinah Washington and famed R & B singer Brook Benton. This dynamic duo also had a hit with the 1960 recording of "Baby (You've Got What It Takes)." Though Washington died all too young at the age of 39, Aretha Franklin as well as other R & B singers credit her with being a major influence.

Words and Music by
Clyde Otis, Brook Benton and Luchi De Jesus
Arranged by Dan Coates

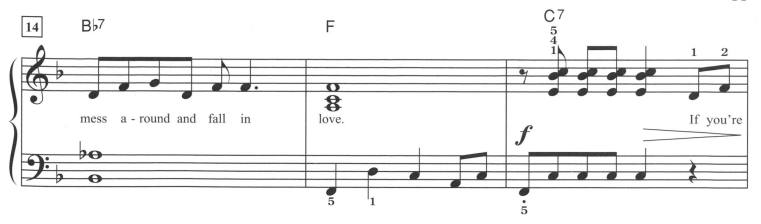

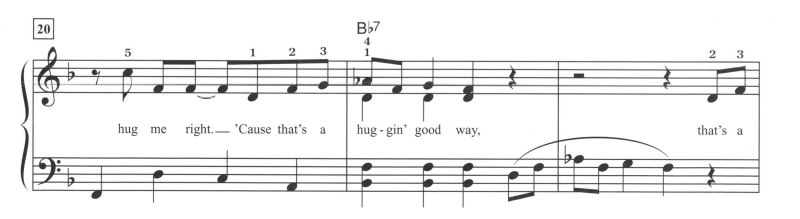

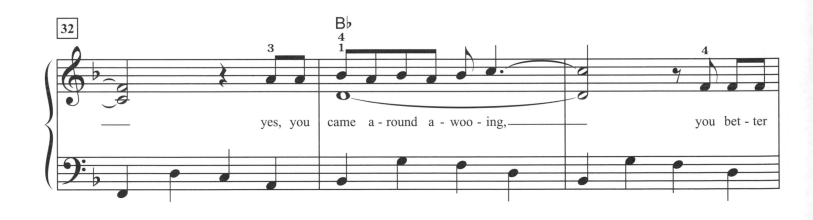

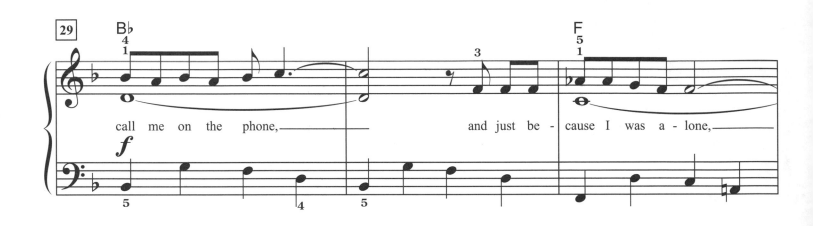

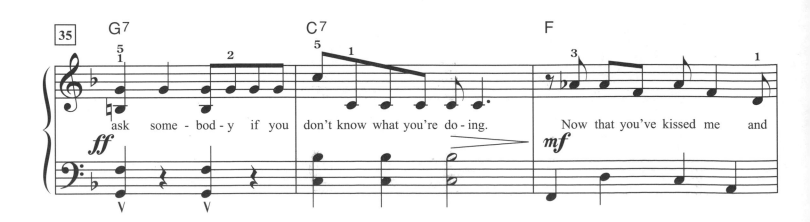

rocked my soul,— don't come a-round knock-in' rock and roll.— 'Cause that's a

rock-in' good way, that's a rock-in' good way,

that's a rock-in' good way to mess a-round and fall in

love. love.

SATIN DOLL

"Satin Doll" was penned by a trifecta of jazz legends: Johnny Mercer, Duke Ellington, and Billy Strayhorn. However, it is believed that all three made their contributions separately. Legend has it that Strayhorn originally wrote the music which was later orchestrated by Ellington. Mercer came into the picture after "Satin Doll" was an established instrumental hit and added lyrics. Since its creation in 1953, it has been recorded by vocal greats including: Ella Fitzgerald, Frank Sinatra, Nancy Wilson, Ramsey Lewis, McCoy Tyner, Nina Simone and Dave Grusin, to name a few.

Words and Music by
Johnny Mercer, Duke Ellington and Billy Strayhorn
Arranged by Dan Coates

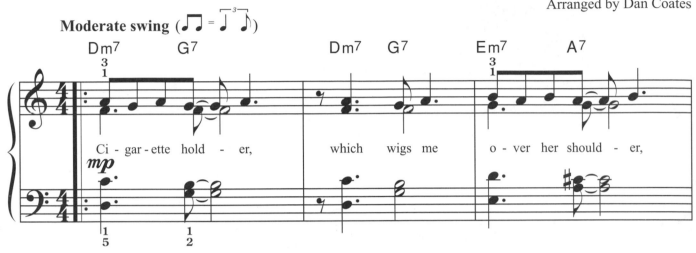

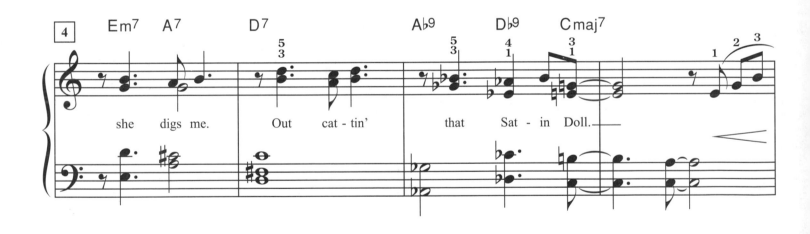

you're flip-pin'. Speaks Lat-in, that Sat - in Doll.

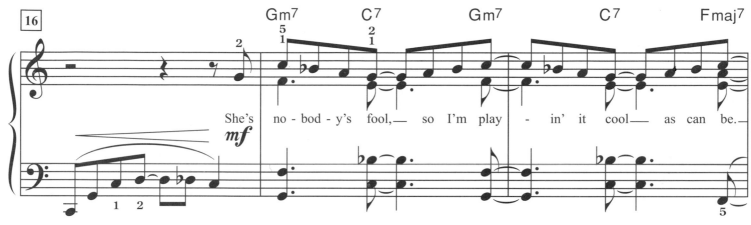

She's no-bod-y's fool,— so I'm play - in' it cool— as can be.

— I'll give it a whirl,— but I ain't—

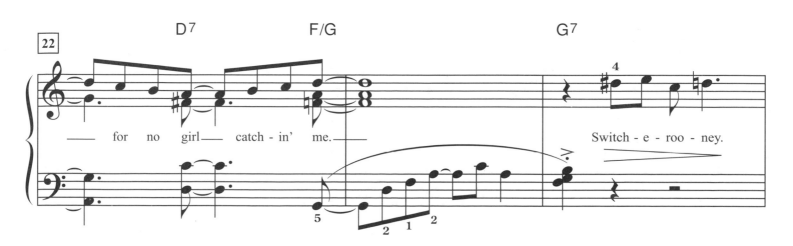

— for no girl— catch-in' me.— Switch - e - roo - ney.

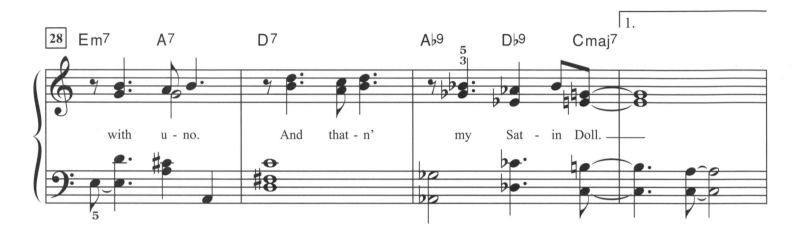

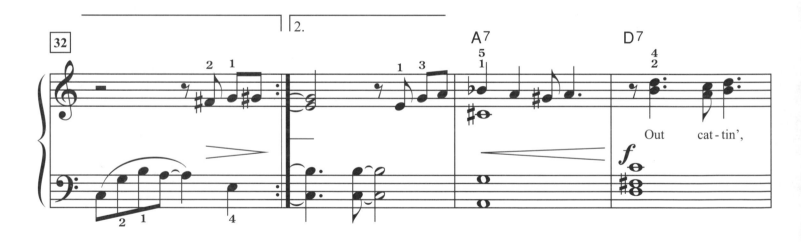

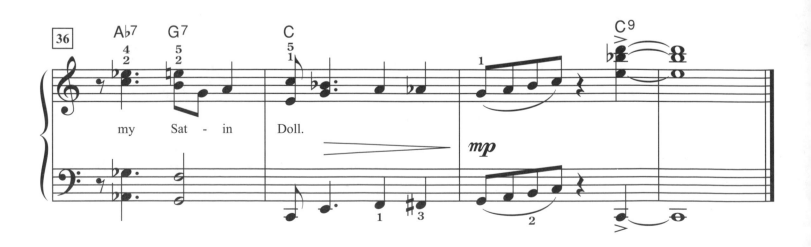

10/6/14

SEE YOU IN SEPTEMBER

"See You in September" is the most well-known song from the 1960s pop group The Happenings. Penned in 1959, "See You in September" didn't hit the pop charts until 1966. Other hits from the group include a cover of George Gershwin's "I Got Rhythm," "Go Away Little Girl," "My Mammy," "Hare Krishna" (from the musical *Hair*), and "Girl on a Swing." The Happenings are still performing today, however lead singer Bob Miranda is the only original member still in the group.

Words by Sid Wayne
Music by Sherman Edwards
Arranged by Dan Coates

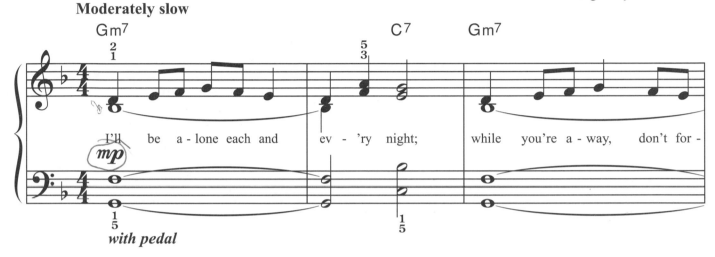

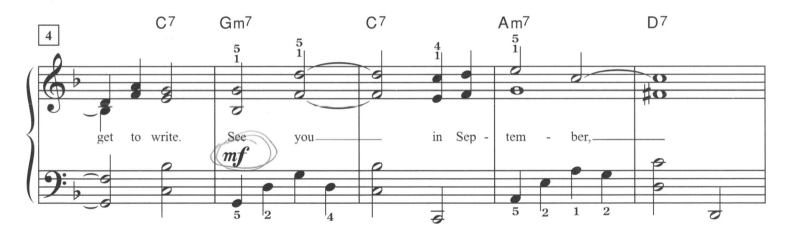

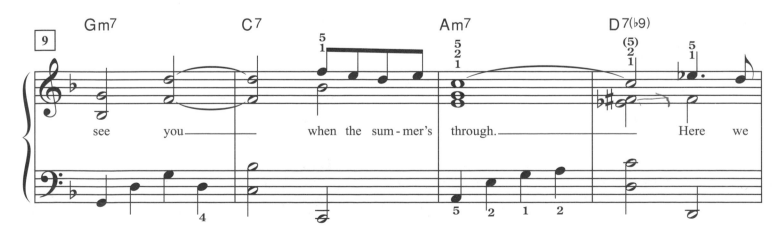

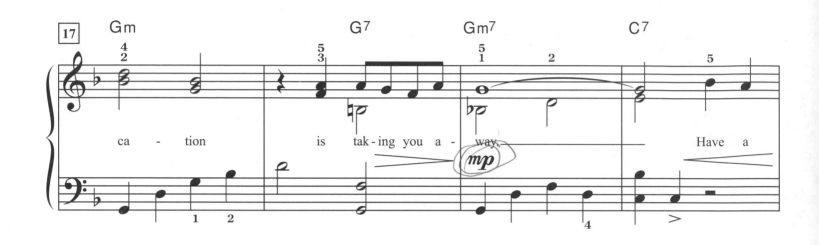

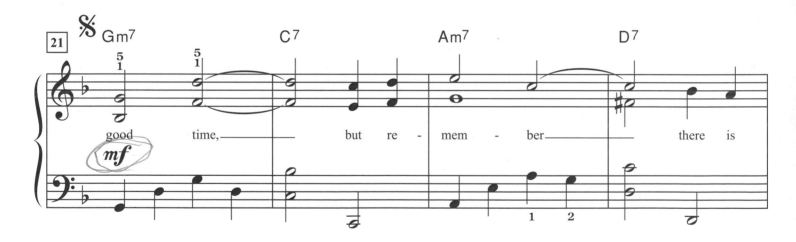

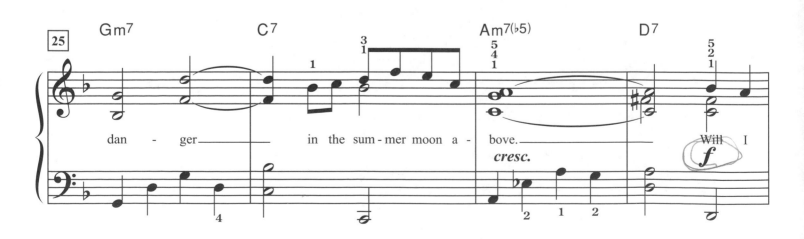

SH-BOOM
(LIFE COULD BE A DREAM)

"Sh-Boom" is considered by many to be the first, well-known doo-wop song. Doo-wop was a style of vocal music made popular in the 1950s. It takes its name from the nonsense syllables that are sung (like "sh-boom"). The original version hit #3 on the R & B charts and #9 on the pop charts. The most famous version is by The Crew Cuts who performed "Sh-Boom" on the Ed Sullivan show. Their version hit #1 on the Billboard charts in 1954.

Words and Music by
James Keyes, Carl Feaster, Floyd McRae,
Claude Feaster and James Edwards
Arranged by Dan Coates

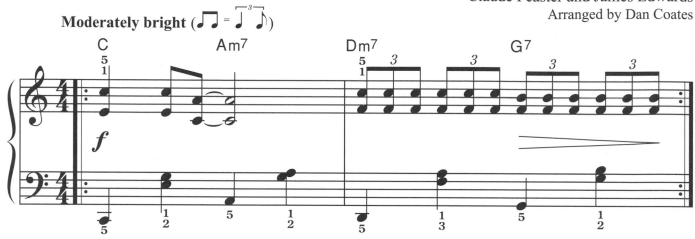

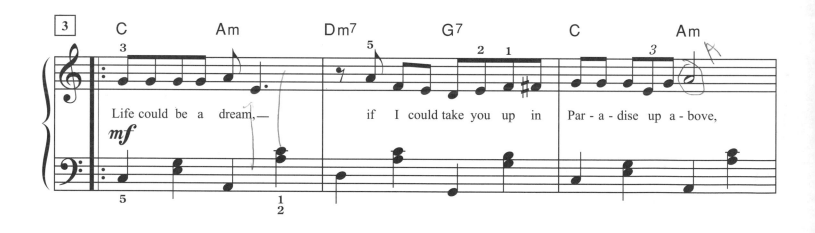

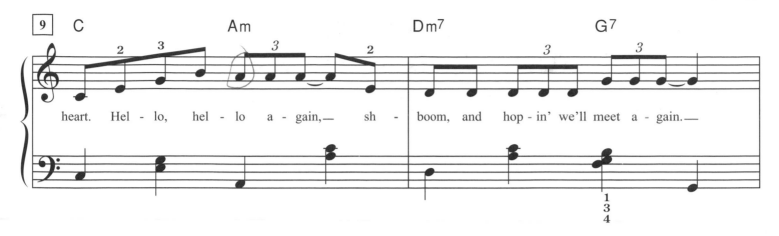

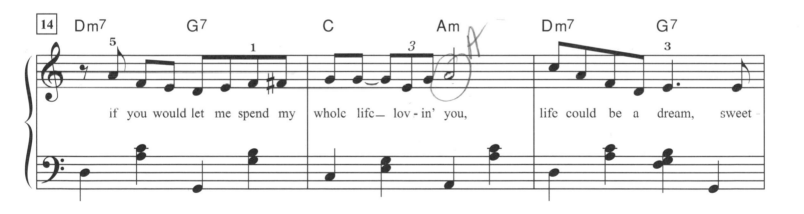

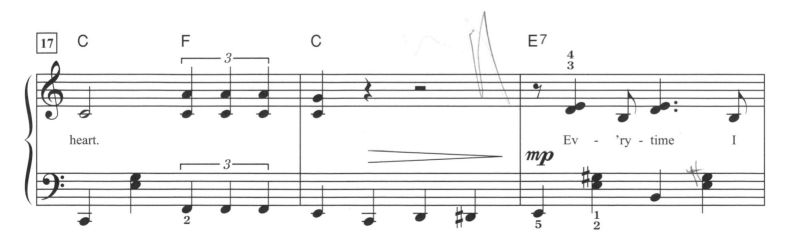

look at you,—— some - thing is on my mind.——

If you'd do what I want you to,—— ba - by, we'd be so

fine. Oh, life could be a dream,— if I could take you up in

Par - a - dise up a - bove, if you would tell me I'm the on - ly one that you love,

SIXTEEN CANDLES

"Sixteen Candles" is the biggest hit from the popular 1950s group The Crests. It reached #2 on the Billboard charts in 1958. In addition to "Sixteen Candles," The Crests had several Top 40 hits including "Step By Step," "Trouble in Paradise," and "The Angels Listened In." A rarity at that time, The Crests were a racially integrated group with two African-American members, one Puerto Rican, and one Italian. In 2004, they were inducted into The Vocal Group Hall of Fame.

Words and Music by
Luther Dixon and Allyson Khent
Arranged by Dan Coates

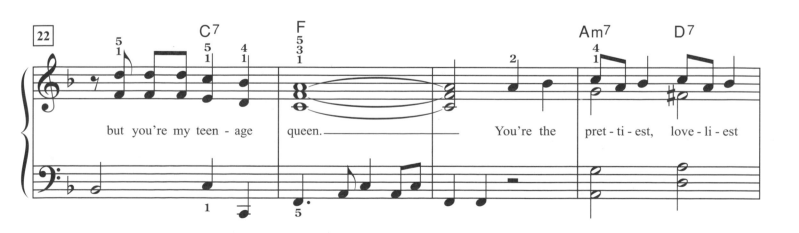

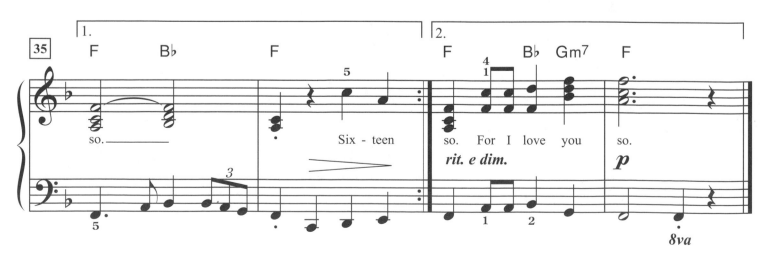

1/18/12

THAT'S ENTERTAINMENT

"That's Entertainment" was written for the 1953 musical film *The Band Wagon*. There are numerous performances of the song throughout the movie by Fred Astaire, Oscar Levant, and others. Since being published in 1953, it has become a theme for Hollywood and the entertainment business alongside classics such as "There's No Business Like Show Business" and "Hooray for Hollywood."

Words by Howard Dietz
Music by Arthur Schwartz
Arranged by Dan Coates

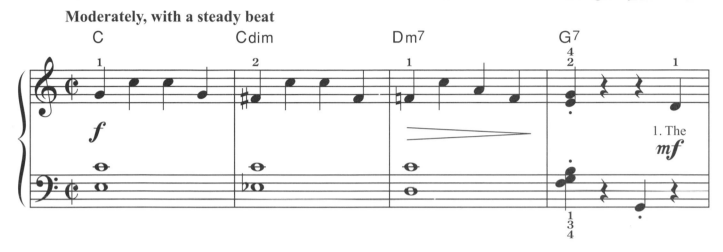

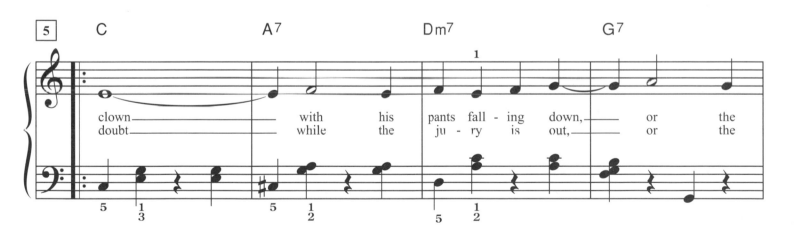

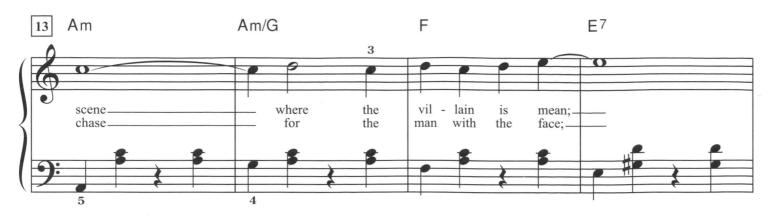

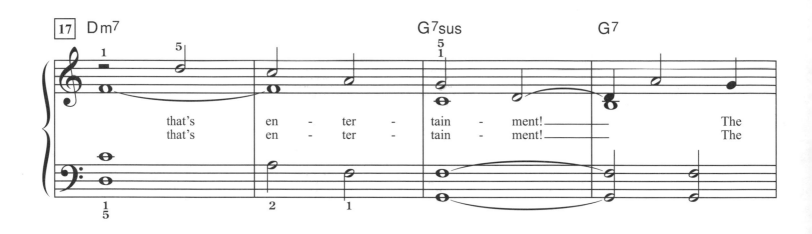

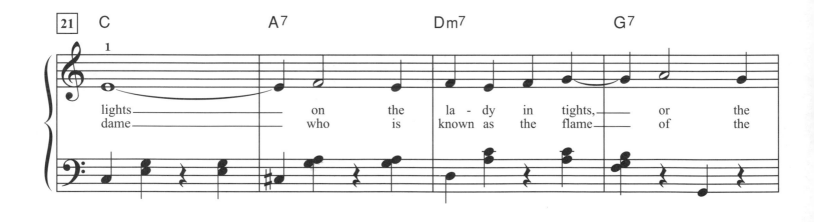

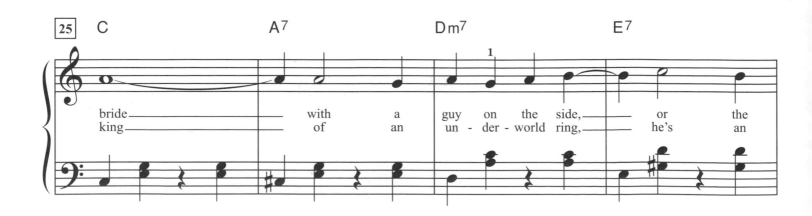

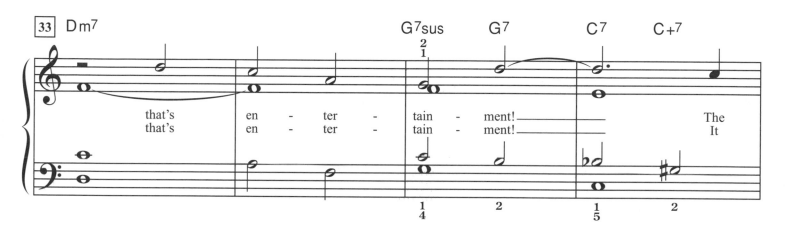

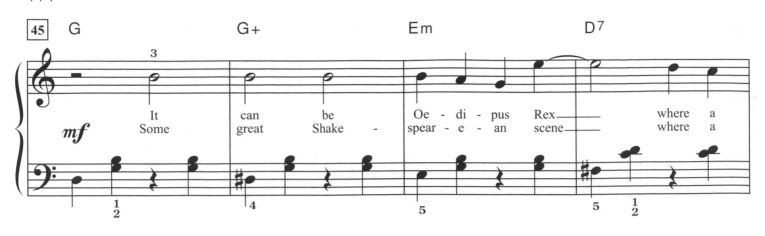

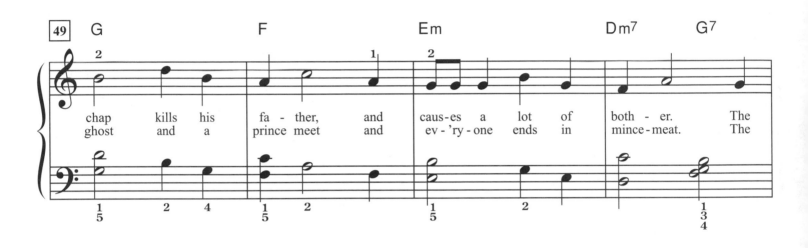

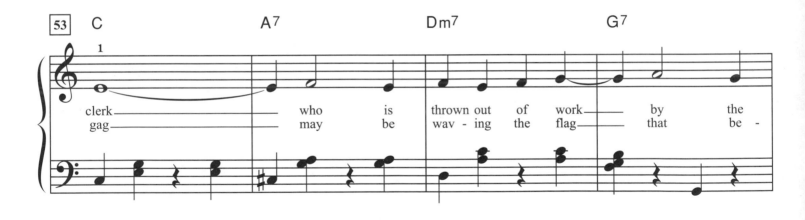

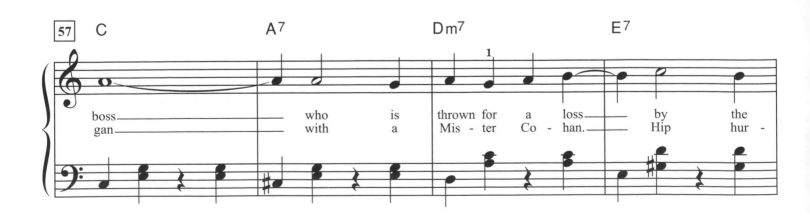

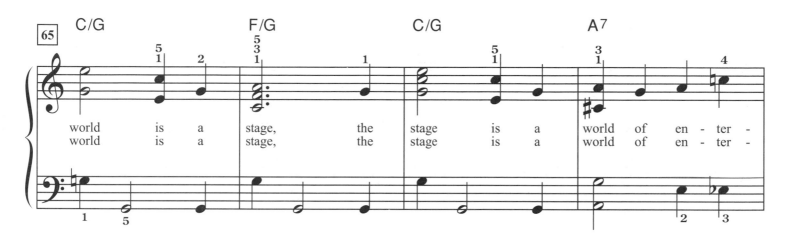

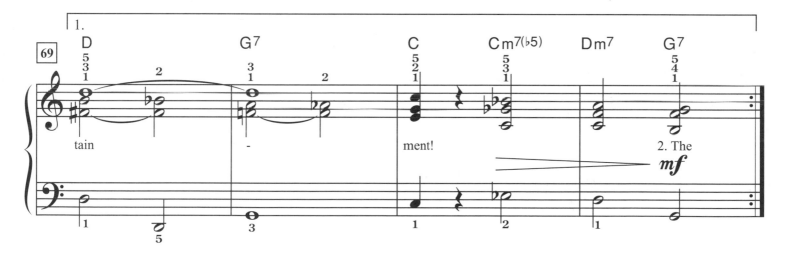

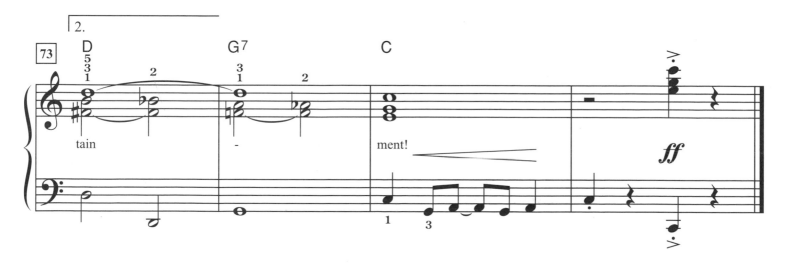

THANK HEAVEN FOR LITTLE GIRLS

"Thank Heaven for Little Girls" is the first number from the musical *Gigi*. Originally a novel by the French author, Collette, *Gigi* has been a play, a musical, and a movie. The 1951 play starred a then-unknown Audrey Hepburn, who went on to win a Theatre World Award for her performance. The 1958 movie won nine Academy Awards including Best Picture of the Year. The 1973 musical won a Tony Award for Best Original Score.

Lyrics by Alan Jay Lerner
Music by Frederick Loewe
Arranged by Dan Coates

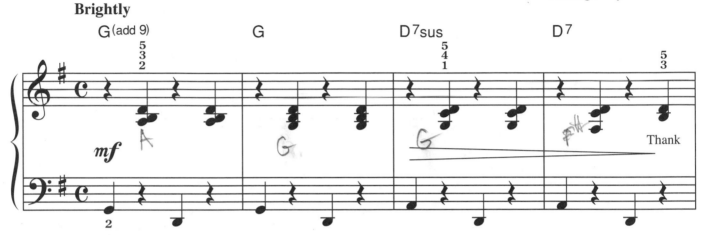

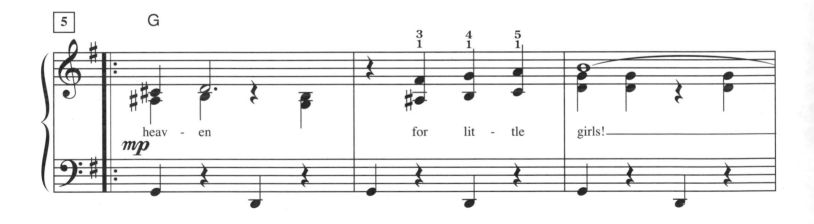

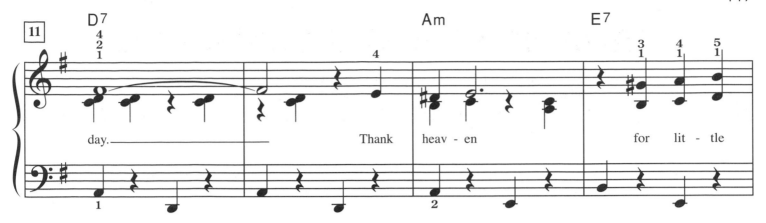

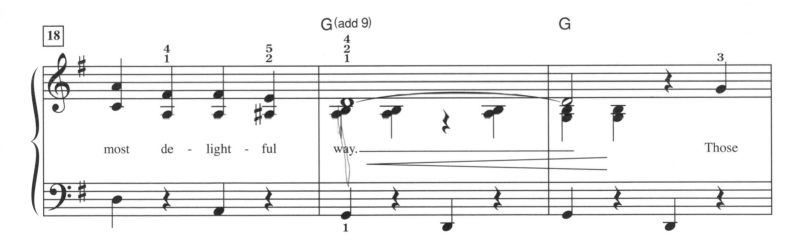

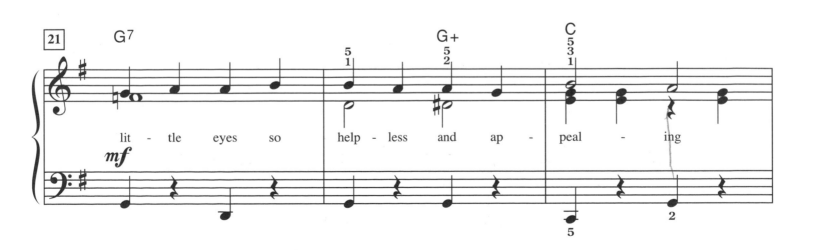

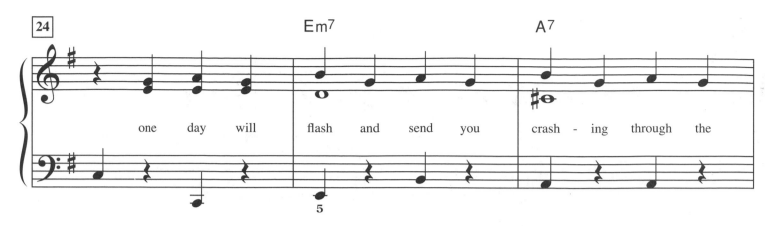

one day will flash and send you crash - ing through the

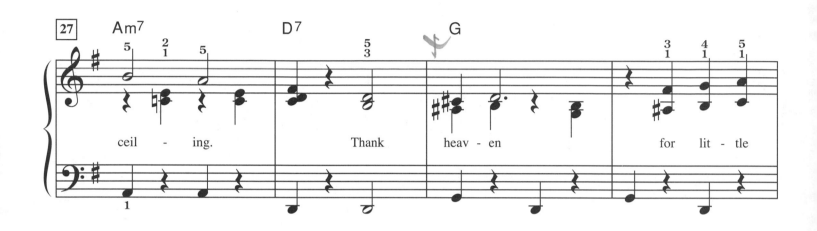

ceil - ing. Thank heav - en for lit - tle

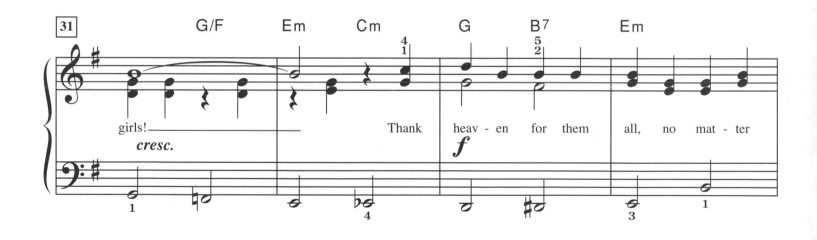

girls! _____ Thank heav - en for them all, no mat - ter

cresc.

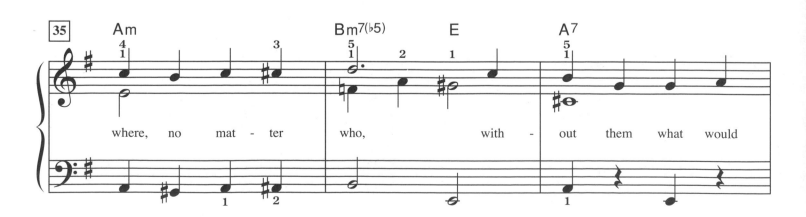

where, no mat - ter who, with - out them what would

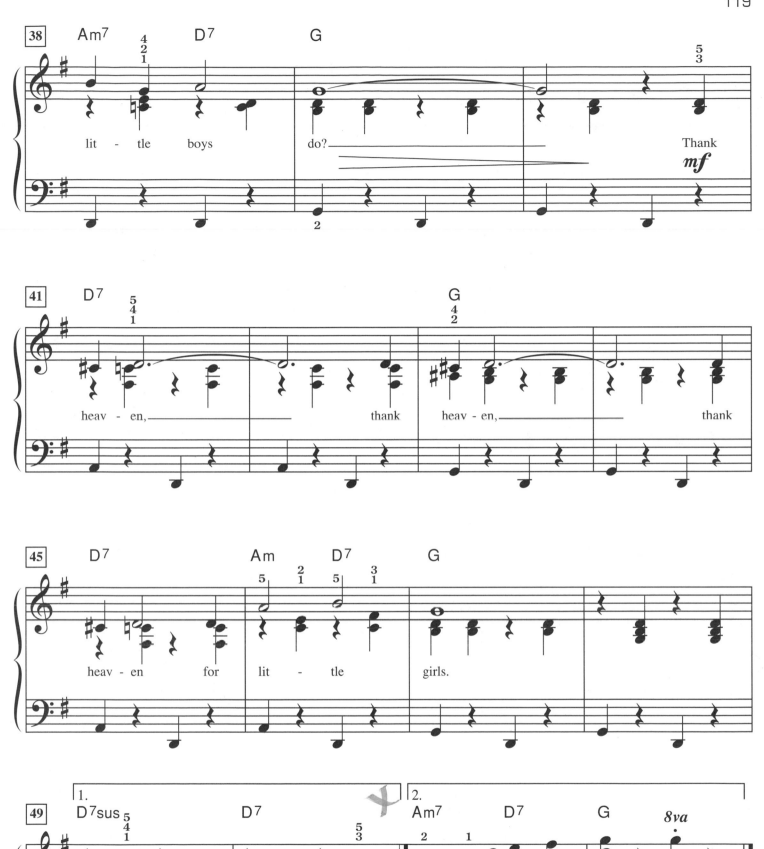

7/14/11

THEME FROM "A SUMMER PLACE"

"Theme from 'A Summer Place'" was featured in the 1959 movie *A Summer Place*, starring Sandra Dee and Troy Donahue. It holds the distinction of being the first movie theme to win a Grammy Award for Record of the Year. It also is the longest-running instrumental hit; the Percy Faith recording stayed at #1 for nine weeks and was the best-selling single of the year. Interestingly, the Percy Faith recording was not used in the movie. Instead, Hugo Winterhalter's recording was used.

Words by Mack Discant
Music by Max Steiner
Arranged by Dan Coates

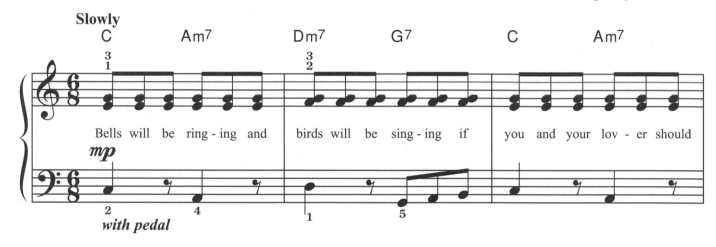

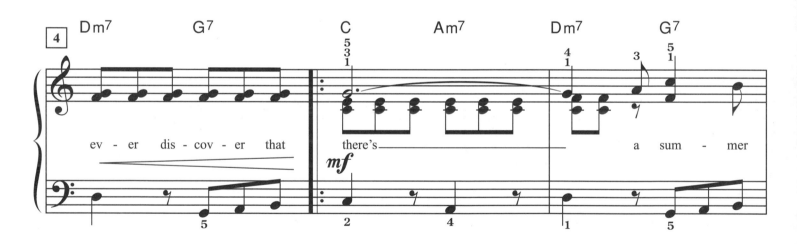

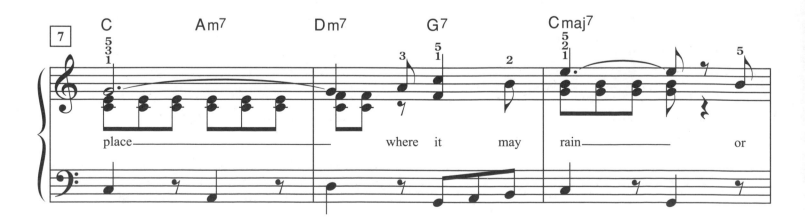

© 1960 (Renewed) WB MUSIC CORP.
All Rights Reserved

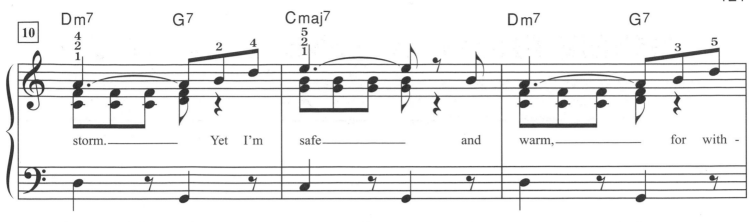

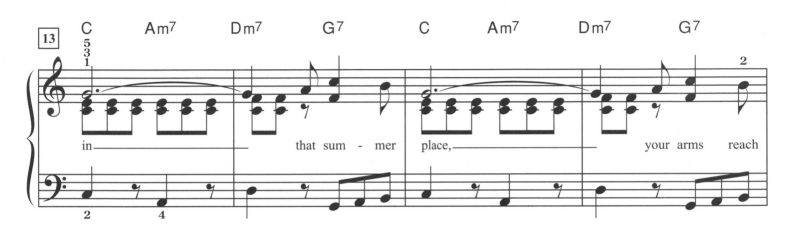

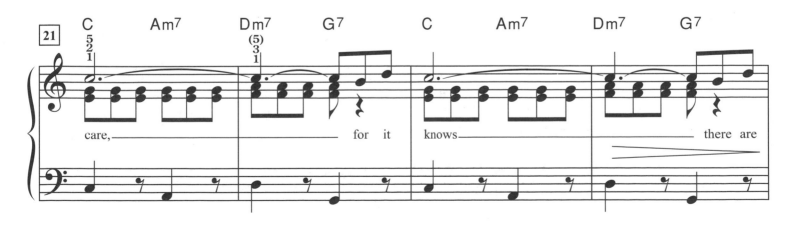

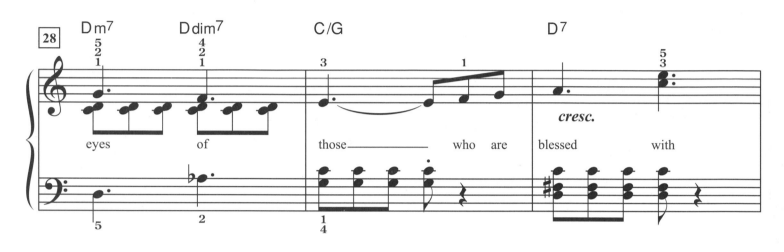

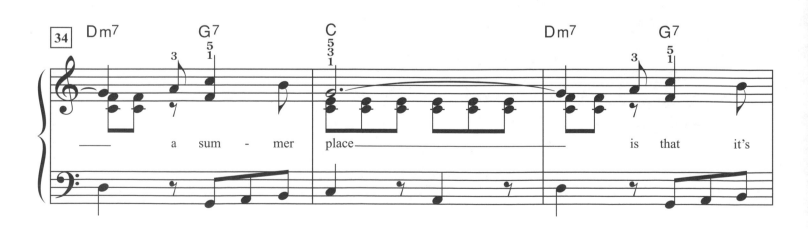

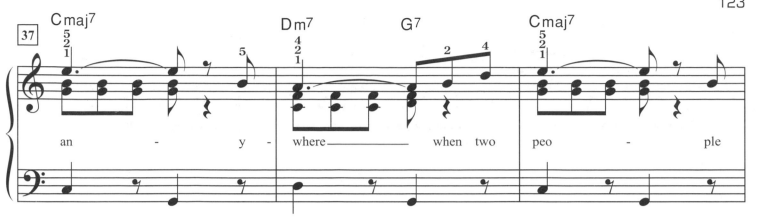

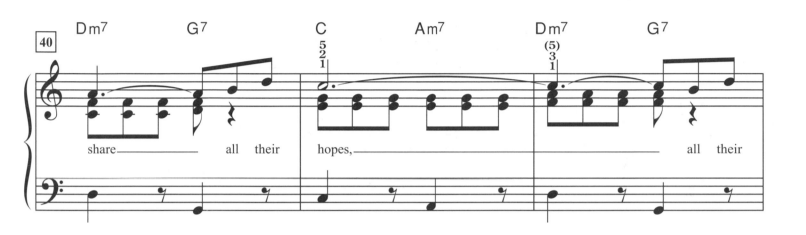

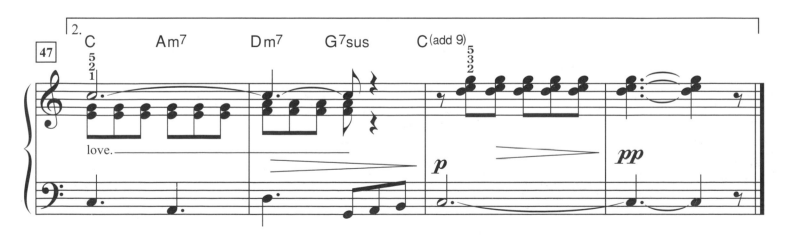

11/29/12

THIS BITTER EARTH

"This Bitter Earth" was made famous by Dinah Washington. (Another Washington hit, "A Rockin' Good Way," is on page 94.) "This Bitter Earth" was a huge hit for Washington and topped both the R & B and Pop charts. Nearly 20 years after its initial publication, it was used in the 1977 film *Killer Sheep*, directed by Charles Burnett. The movie takes a close look at African-American culture in Los Angeles' Watts district.

Words and Music by Clyde Otis
Arranged by Dan Coates

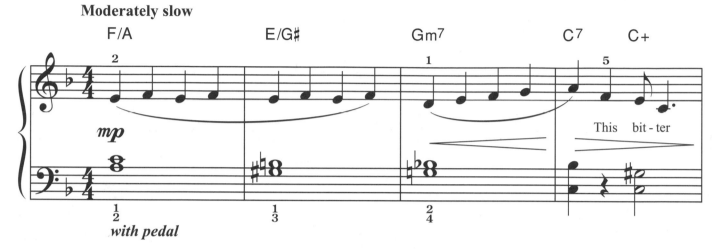

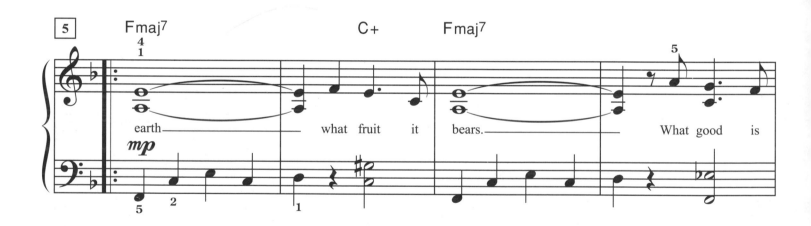

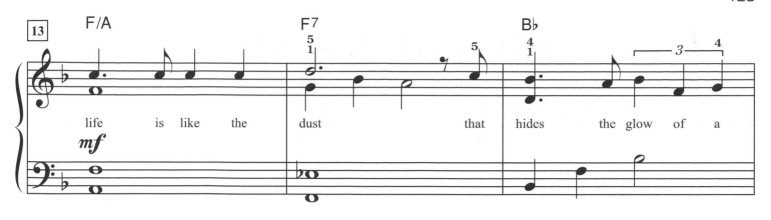

life   is   like   the   dust   that   hides   the   glow   of   a

mf

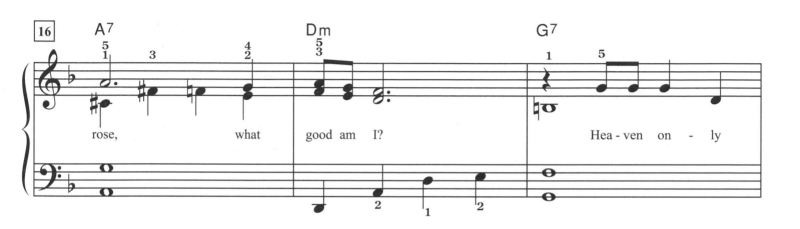

rose,   what   good   am   I?   Hea - ven   on - ly

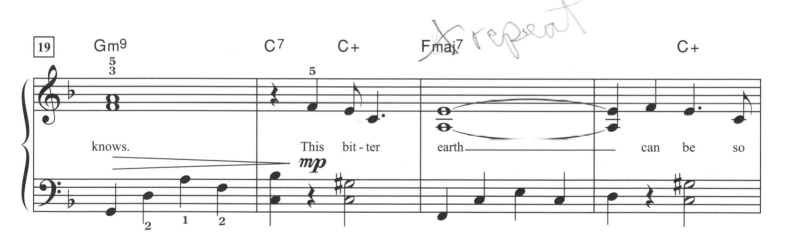

✗ repeat

knows.   This   bit - ter   earth——————   can   be   so

mp

cold;———————   to - day   you're   young——————   too   soon   you're

cresc.

old._____ But while a voice with-in me

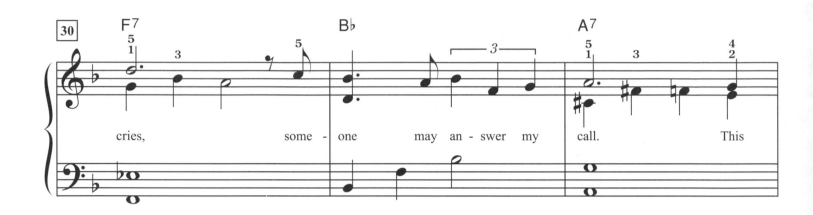

cries, some - one may an-swer my call. This

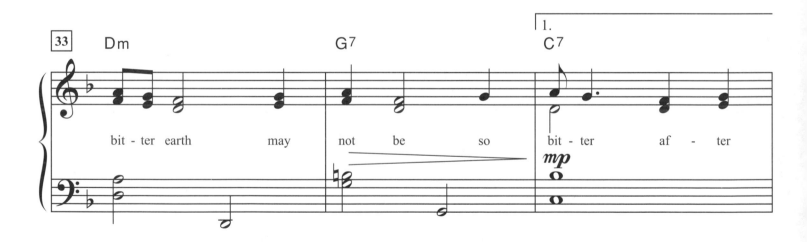

bit-ter earth may not be so bit-ter af - ter

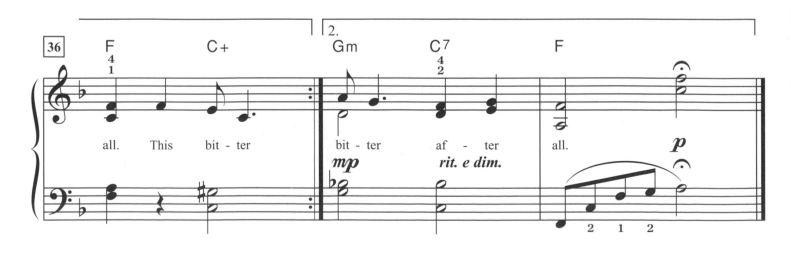

all. This bit-ter bit-ter af - ter all.

TILL

"Till" found its way onto the pop charts in three different decades. In the 1950s, Percy Faith and Roger Williams both scored hits with this standard. In the 1960s, Tony Bennett, Shirley Bassey, The Angels, Bobby Vinton, and The Vogues all hit the charts with their versions. In 1970 and 1971, respectively, the Welsh singers Dorothy Squires and Tom Jones each had hits with "Till."

English Words by Carl Sigman
Music by Charles Danvers
Arranged by Dan Coates

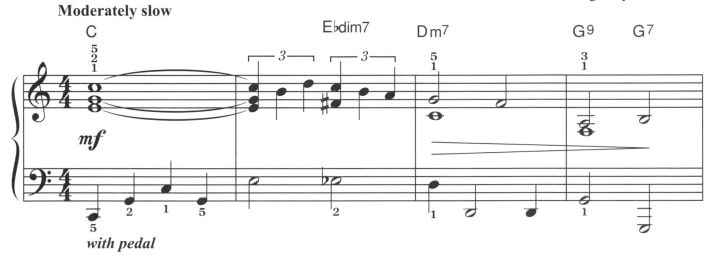

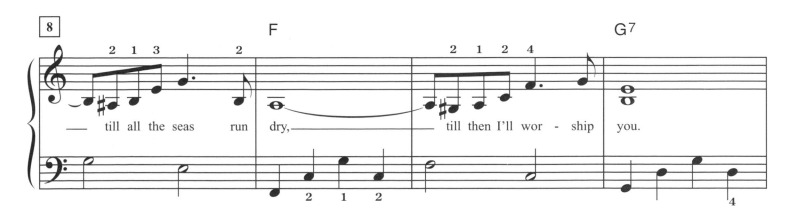

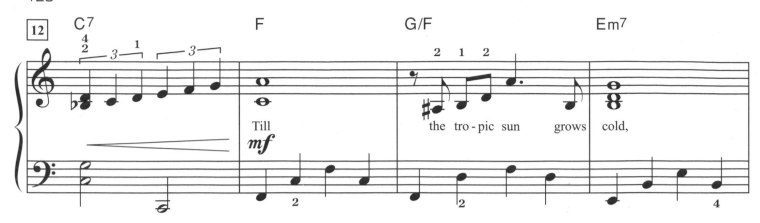

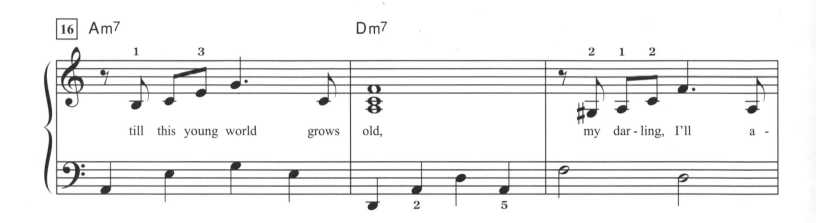

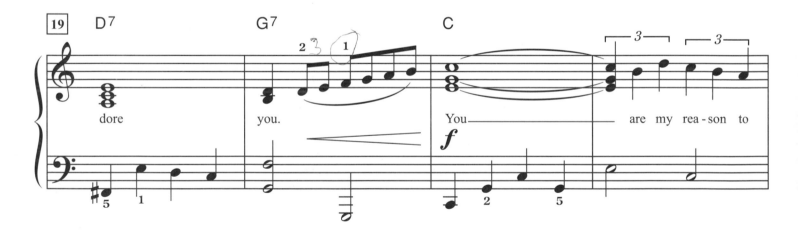

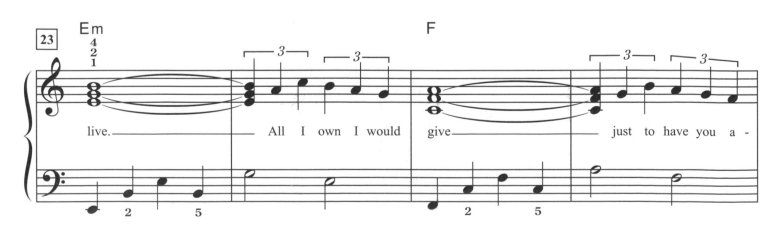

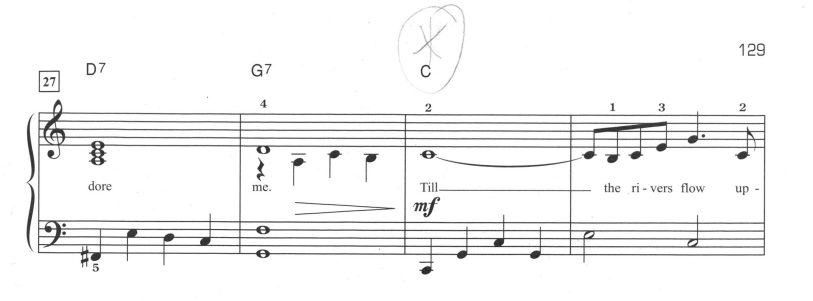

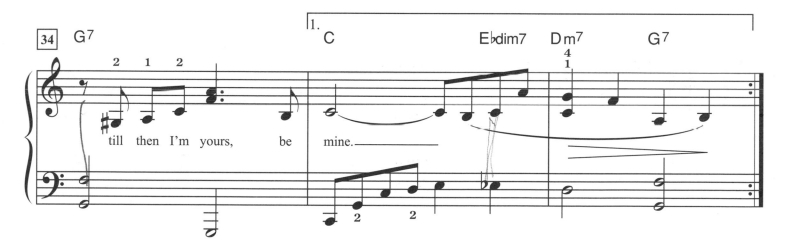

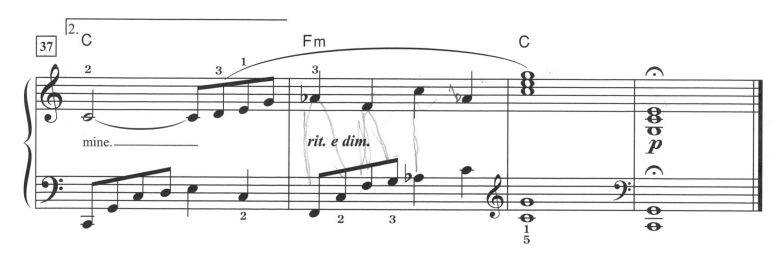

TOGETHER, WHEREVER WE GO

"Together, Wherever We Go" is from the 1959 musical *Gypsy*, which is based on the 1957 memoirs of Gypsy Rose Lee, a striptease artist. Lee's mother, Mama Rose, is central to the plot and is considered the ultimate "stage mother." Other popular songs from *Gypsy* include "All I Need Is the Girl," "Everything's Coming up Roses," "You Gotta Get a Gimmick," and "Let Me Entertain You."

Lyrics by Stephen Sondheim
Music by Jule Styne
Arranged by Dan Coates

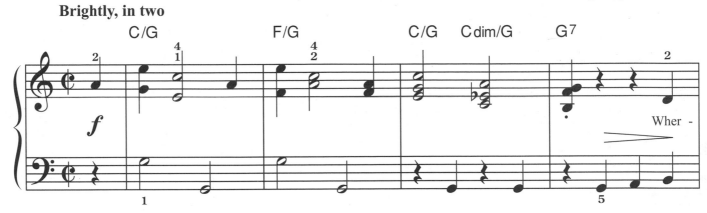

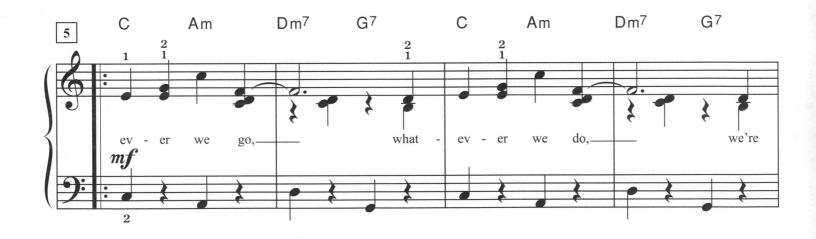

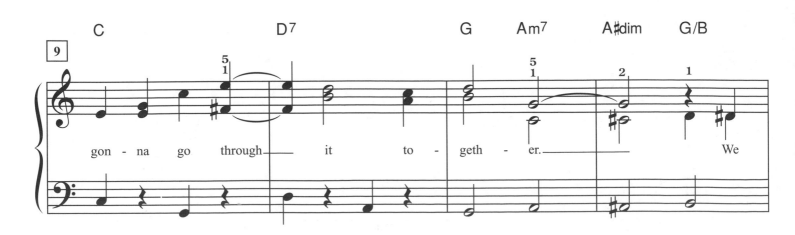

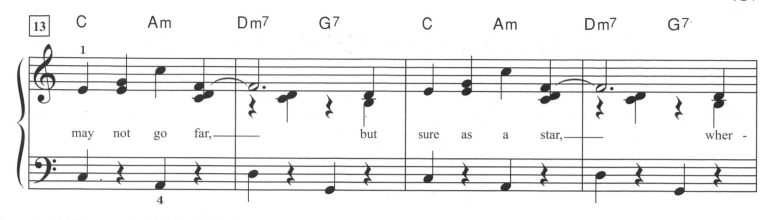

may not go far,——— but sure as a star,——— wher-

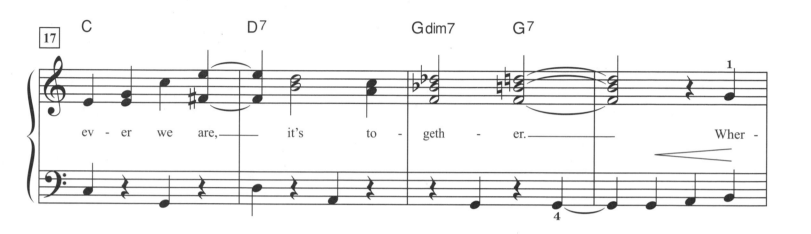

ev - er we are,——— it's to - geth - er.——— Wher-

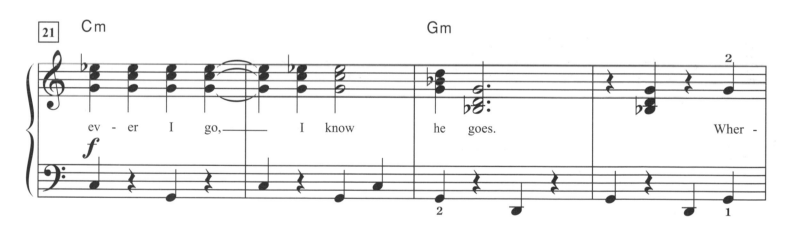

ev - er I go,——— I know he goes. Wher-

ev - er I go,——— I know she goes.

28

No fits, no fights, no feuds and no

31

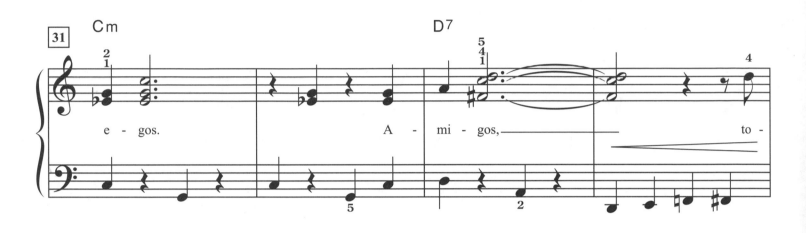

e - gos. A - mi - gos,———— to-

35

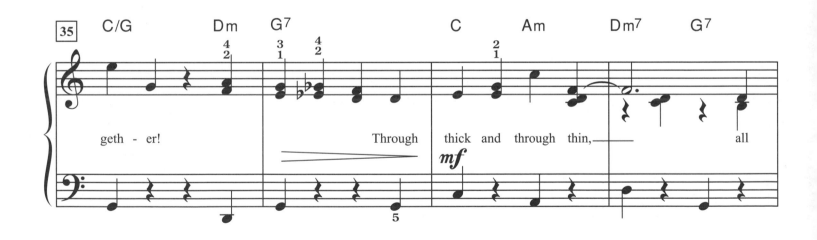

geth - er! Through thick and through thin,———— all

39

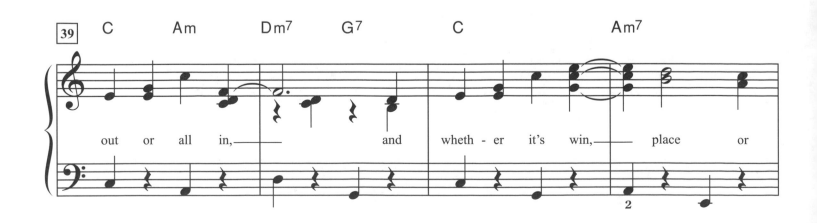

out or all in,———— and wheth - er it's win,———— place or

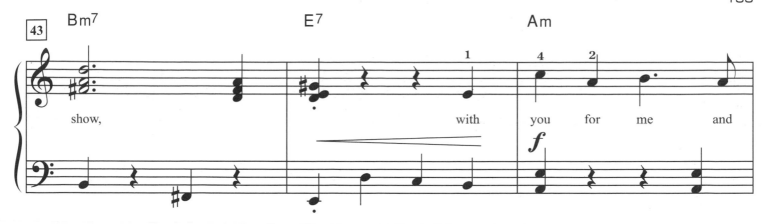

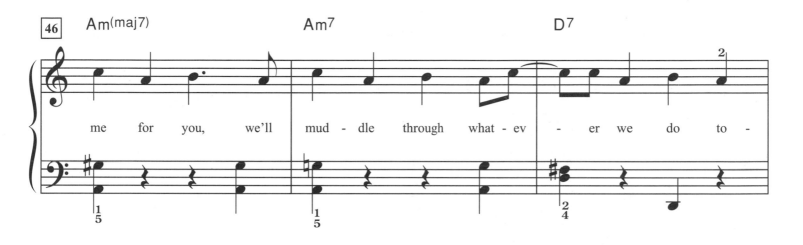

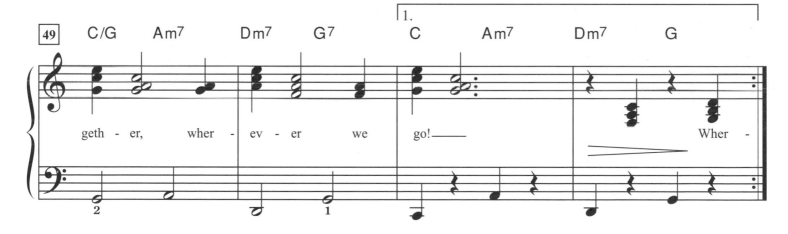

VOLARE
(NEL BLU, DIPINTO DI BLU)

"Volare (nel blu, dipinto di blu)" is Italian for "to fly in the blue painted blue." The composer, Domenico Modugno, received top honors for "Volare" from The Eurovision Song Contest (a European award, similar to the Grammys), Grammy Awards in the U. S., and from Billboard Magazine Best Singer, Best Song, and Best Album. Countless artists have recorded "Volare" including: Dean Martin, Bobby Rydell, and The Gipsy Kings.

English Lyric by Mitchell Parish
Original Italian Text by D. Modugno and F. Migliacci

Music by Domenico Modugno
Arranged by Dan Coates

WALKIN' MY BABY BACK HOME

"Walkin' My Baby Back Home" enjoyed a life on the charts in three consecutive decades. It first hit the pop charts in 1931, and in 1945 the popular singer Jo Stafford recorded a version. However, it is the Nat King Cole version (released in 1951) that is the biggest hit of them all. It was also the title song from the 1953 film starring Donald O'Connor, Janet Leigh, Buddy Hackett, and Scatman Crothers. This movie marked Buddy Hackett's film debut.

Words and Music by Fred E. Ahlert and Roy Turk
Arranged by Dan Coates

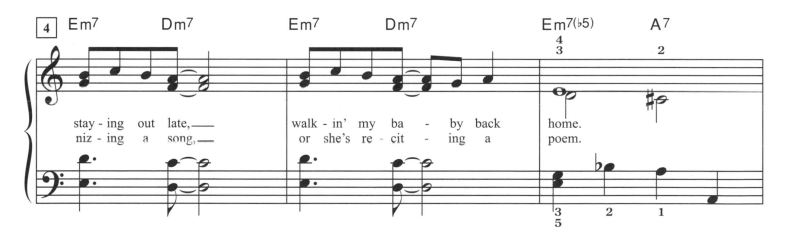

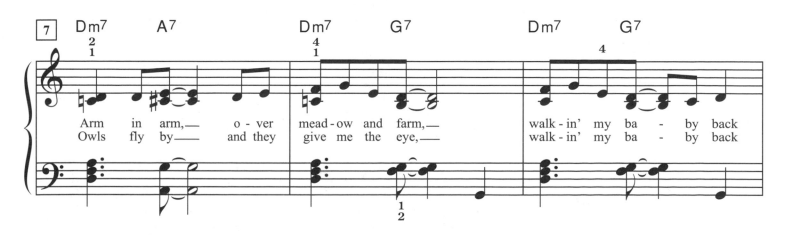

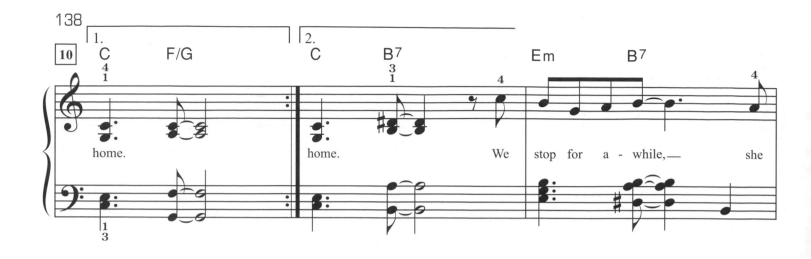

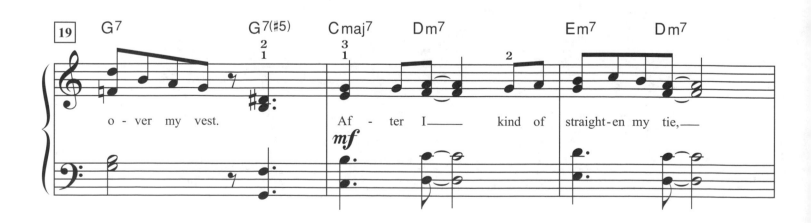

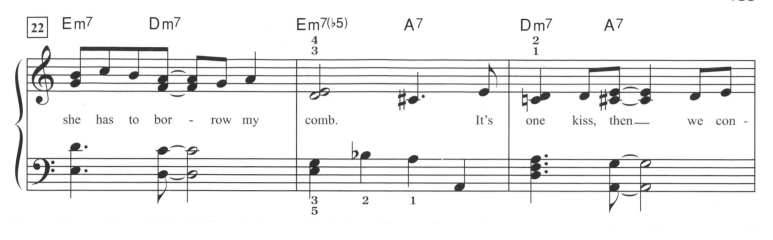

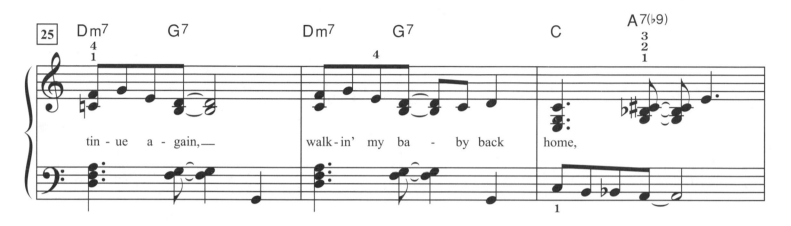

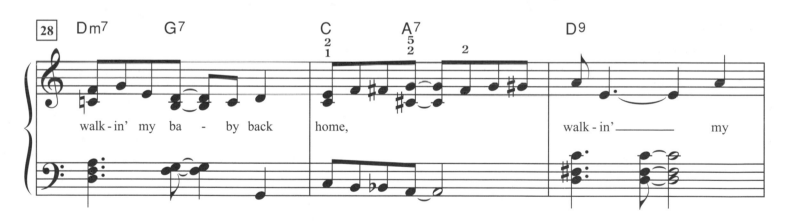

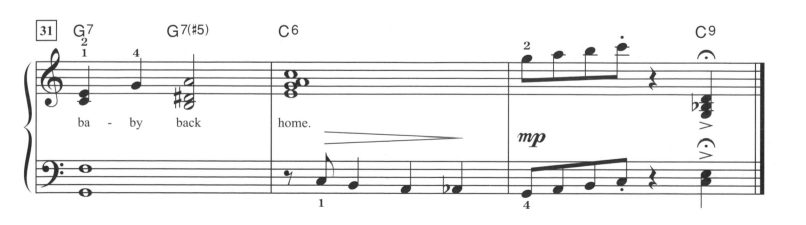

4/5/12

(WE'RE GONNA) ROCK AROUND THE CLOCK

"(We're Gonna) Rock Around the Clock" is considered the first rock and roll song. The most famous version was recorded by Bill Haley & His Comets in 1954. However, it did not hit the pop charts until it played during the opening credits of the 1955 film *Blackboard Jungle*. Following its film "debut," it topped the American Billboard charts for eight weeks.

Words and Music by
Max C. Freedman and Jimmy De Knight
Arranged by Dan Coates

WHO'S SORRY NOW

9/20/12

"Who's Sorry Now" was published in 1923 and featured in the 1946 Marx Brothers film *A Night in Casablanca*. However, its true fame came from the 1958 version by Connie Francis which earned a gold record for reaching one million copies in sales. Other Connie Francis hits include "Where the Boys Are" and "Everybody's Somebody's Fool."

Music by Ted Snyder
Words by Bert Kalmar and Harry Ruby
Arranged by Dan Coates

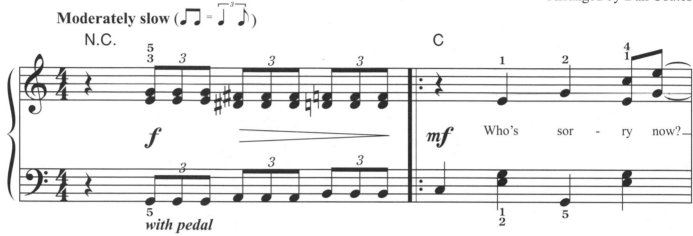

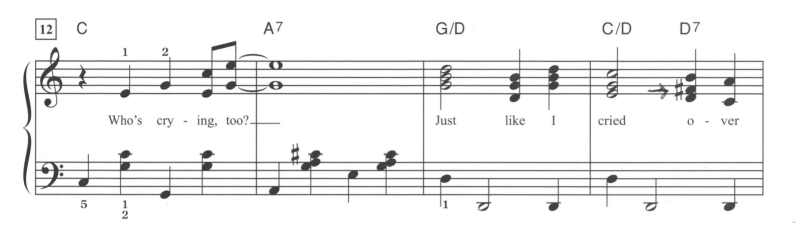

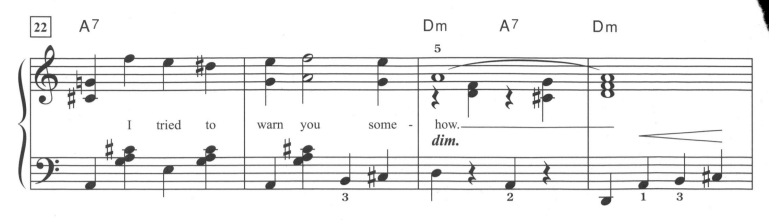

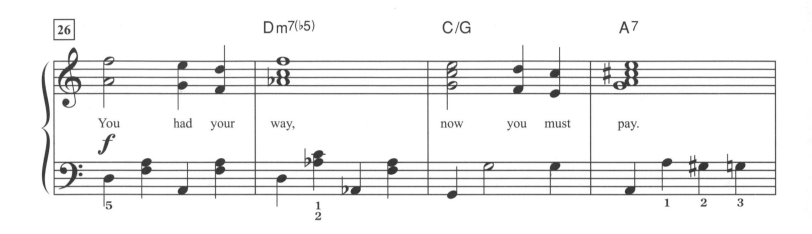

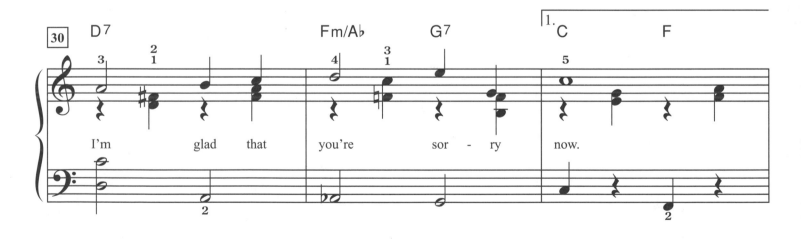

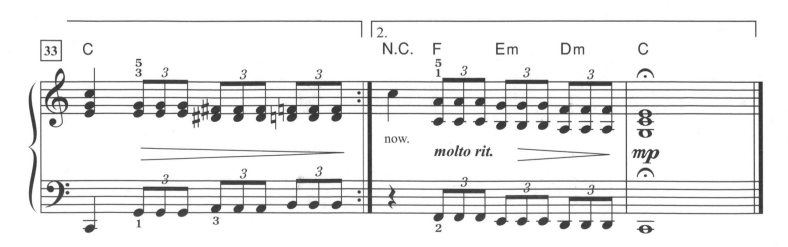